# WISDOM AT THE CROSSROADS

## THE LIFE & THOUGHT OF
## MICHAEL PAUL GALLAGHER SJ

THOMAS G. CASEY SJ

Published by Messenger Publications, 2018

ISBN 978 1 910248 89 8

Designed by Messenger Publications Design Department
Typeset in Baskerville and Trajan
Printed by W&G Baird Ltd

Messenger Publications,
37 Lower Leeson Street, Dublin D02 W938
www.messenger.ie

*Wherever in the Church, even in the most difficult and extreme fields, at the crossroads of ideologies, in the social trenches, there has been and there is confrontation between the burning exigencies of the human being and the perennial message of the Gospel, there also there have been, and there are, Jesuits.*

Pope Paul VI (Address to General Congregation 34, 1974)

## DEDICATION

*It has been a privilege to live alongside many Jesuits whose glad gratitude is always bursting into flower, making them taste the fragrance of goodness in most places and nearly all of the time. This book is dedicated to them.*

## BOOKS BY MICHAEL PAUL GALLAGHER SJ

*Help My Unbelief*

*Free to Believe: Ten Steps to Faith*

*Struggles of Faith*

*Where is Your God?*

*What Will Give Us Happiness?*

*Letters on Prayer*

*What Are They Saying about Unbelief?*

*Questions of Faith*

*Clashing Symbols: An Introduction to Faith and Culture*

*Will our Children Believe?*

*Dive Deeper: The Human Poetry of Faith*

*The Disturbing Freshness of Christ*

*Faith Maps: Ten Religious Explorers from Newman to Joseph Ratzinger*

*Into Extra Time: Living through the Final Stages of Cancer and Jottings along the Way*

# TABLE OF CONTENTS

# ACKNOWLEDGEMENTS

I'm thankful to the late Fr Michael Paul Gallagher SJ; without his life and thought, this book would obviously never have been written.

I'd like to thank Fr Patrick Carberry SJ, Editor at Messenger Publications, for encouraging me to take on this project, and for his invaluable feedback and comments as the script took shape.

I am grateful to the Holy Spirit, who touched my memory, my understanding and my will in unexpected ways. I used to have misgivings about St Ignatius Loyola's prayer, *Take, Lord, receive all my liberty, my memory, my understanding, and my entire will.* Did it mean that I'd be left with nothing? Writing this book, I've discovered the opposite: my memory, understanding and will have been sharpened, enabling me to recall essential aspects of Michael Paul's thought, inspiring me to ask important questions, and guiding me to choose topics that should prove helpful. I hope you'll find evidence of this in the pages that follow.

# FOREWORD

This is a remarkable book, coming from two remarkable Jesuits. Both very cultured persons – in the richest sense of that term – with a mastery of many modern and ancient languages, they were colleagues for ten years at the Gregorian University in Rome. They thought deeply about faith, the challenges of unbelief and atheism, and the control that a runaway, modern society exercises on a generation with fewer roots and bigger pressures. Both these Irish Jesuits have reflected long and hard on the shift from a culture where it was almost impossible not to believe, at least in some rudimentary fashion, to a culture where we must constantly struggle to open ourselves to adult faith and to maintain it.

Blessed with first-rate writing skills, they could produce not only valuable academic works but could also dive deeper into people's emotions and imagination, and so stir wonder that, in an imaginative and poetic way, kept their readers on the journey of faith or set them on it for the first time. Now dean of philosophy at St Patrick's College, Maynooth, Tom Casey enjoys intellectual and spiritual gifts that make him match and complement those of the late Michael Paul Gallagher. It was a decision of genius to select him as the historian and interpreter of Michael Paul's spiritual pilgrimage and ministry.

Part of that pilgrimage belonged to the years when, from 1990, Michael Paul worked for the Pontifical Council of Culture under Cardinal Paul Poupard. Some influential people at the Vatican had invited Michael Paul to set aside something of his adventurous dialogue with the contemporary world and 'sit on our own side of the table'. They clearly hinted at promotion to a bishopric within the Vatican or back home in Ireland, but Michael Paul would have none of it. Such a curb on the freedom and growth of his specific vocation – which he saw as helping people get in touch with the real God by getting in touch with their real selves, what Tom Casey calls his 'ministry of consolation' – was unacceptable to him.

Michael Paul's influence as an outstanding teacher, author and spiritual guide lives on – through his writing, of course, and perhaps even more through the multitude of people whom he taught in Dublin, Rome and elsewhere. They include Antonio Spadaro SJ, the current editor of *Civiltà Cattolica*. Michael Paul directed his master's thesis and examined his doctoral thesis, both of which were on the quest for faith of a modern Italian novelist who died from Aids.

Michael Paul's capacity to detect the marvellous mystery at the heart of seemingly ordinary lives recalls the words of G. K. Chesterton: 'The world will never starve for want of wonders, but for want of wonder'. Michael Paul's own life exemplifies the account a great Presbyterian theologian, Frederick Buechner, gave of vocation: 'The place where God calls you is the place where your deep gladness and the world's deep hunger meet.'

I cannot recommend this book too highly, and feel extremely honoured to be associated with the story of Michael Paul Gallagher and the continuing work of Tom Casey. It is a beautiful book, about a beautiful person, and written by another truly beautiful person.

Gerald O'Collins, SJ, AC
*Jesuit Theological College,*
*Parkville, Australia.*

# UNIQUE INTELLECTUAL

A passion of my life has been to make faith real for people, especially those who find themselves far from Church language or what they once knew as religion. *Into Extra Time*

The idea of 'theology' may ring all the wrong bells for you. It can seem a field of hair-splitting irrelevance. But at its best the job of theology has always been to ponder, pray and incarnate God's Word for now, for many different 'nows'. It is an art of the crossroads, standing in-between, receiving a revelation and translating it. Its call is to mediate God's meaning for us. *Faith Maps*

This book is written in the belief that we can still benefit from the wisdom of the gifted Irish Jesuit, Fr Michael Paul Gallagher, who died in November 2015. By paying particular attention to Michael Paul's thought, this book is more of an intellectual biography than a biography proper. An 'intellectual biography' doesn't mean that you're in for a dry assessment of his academic achievements, however, or a cerebral analysis of his work. Having a string of academic degrees doesn't make someone an intellectual. Michael Paul was an intellectual, but not in the sense of sitting at a desk in an ivory tower. He was an intellectual because he reflected intelligently about the world and had something worth saying. He said things that made a difference to people's lives, and he provided insights that encouraged them to think and act in a new way.

## Grasping the Bigger Picture

Michael Paul thought in a way that went below the surface to a deeper level, in order to grasp the underlying meaning of things. His thinking also went beyond immediate concerns. He saw the bigger picture, and he took an active part in the large conversations of our day: about what it means to believe or not to believe, about how culture forms and deforms us, and about the decisive role of the imagination in our lives. He never looked at things in isolation, but always made creative links and connections between different areas of thought.

Someone once quipped, 'You can tell an intellectual, but you can't tell him much'. We can be grateful that Michael Paul hadn't that kind of closed mind. He didn't dodge questions. He himself was always questioning, seeking and searching. In fact, he did so until a week before he died: at that point he stopped writing, but only because his thought patterns and speech were becoming confused. Up until then, he loved opening up original questions and new avenues of exploration.

Even though I am concentrating on Michael Paul's intellectual contribution, his thought and life cannot really be separated. Michael Paul was the kind of thinker whose life was always relevant to his thought, because his intellectual concerns were rooted in his lived experience. For that reason, his life won't be overlooked or neglected in this book. Instead I will integrate his particular way of reflecting about culture and reality into the story of who he was. Putting his thought and life side by side will give a fuller and richer picture of the person he was and the impact he had.

## A Powerful Communicator

Michael Paul's insights are worth pondering, not just by priests and ministers, but also by ordinary Christians struggling with how to believe amidst the pressures and complexities of contemporary culture. Michael Paul speaks to today's context. He had his finger on the pulse of our changing culture, helping people to make sense of what it means to be a Christian in this new millennium.

What made Michael Paul a unique intellectual worth listening to? For one thing, he wasn't a one-dimensional intellectual. He never became stuck in a rut. He constantly reinvented himself and his ideas as the years went by. And he didn't say what he said in a boring way, because monotony was anathema to him. He always found gripping ways of communicating his ideas. Even when he returned to an old and familiar theme, he was able to approach it in a fresh way, as though for the first time. He didn't play the same tune over and over again like a broken record; in fact, to change the image slightly, he had many strings to his bow. He had many facets and dimensions as an intellectual and a thinker. Let me list some of these appealing qualities.

First, he was creative. This creativity extended to his style, to the way he wrote and the way he spoke. There was nothing stale or hackneyed about his way of expressing things. Because of his rich background in literature, he presented his insights in a poetic way. His love for literature meant that he could readily draw from writers as varied as George Herbert, Fyodor Dostoevsky, Flannery O'Connor, Saul Bellow, Seamus Heaney and Douglas Coupland.

He was a reconciling thinker, always inclined to search for common ground, to emphasise similarities, and not to become fixated by differences. He did not reduce everything to black-and-white alternatives, but was able to see how different things could coexist in a complementary way. As a rule, he did not engage in debates on contentious issues. He feared these might degenerate into long and fruitless arguments that would only sap his intellectual energy and not really touch or move his hearers and readers. He wanted to get people in touch with their core hungers, knowing that these deepest hungers would focus people on what was most central and most important.

He was a respectful thinker – too respectful to be directive. He didn't give a rigid set of instructions to his readers on how to live the Christian life. Instead he gently provoked them into working out their salvation for themselves. He wasn't into quick fixes or instant answers. Neither did he believe in telling people what they liked to hear. He told them instead, albeit in a soothing way, what they needed to hear.

He was a believing intellectual who kept abreast of secular thought. He was awake to the signs of the times. He saw quicker than most priests and theologians that Irish people were becoming increasingly disenchanted with the institutional Church while at the same time harbouring deep spiritual hungers. This wakeful vigilance was linked to his love for young people. He inspired them and learned a lot from them in his turn. He lived mostly in young Jesuit communities and he taught college students for most of his adult life. There were many things he loved about young people: their fresh perspectives, their openness to new ideas, their intense curiosity, their refusal to accept pat answers, their intuitive grasp of how culture was changing and their spontaneous love of life.

He was a sacramental thinker, by which I mean someone who was convinced that ordinary reality could reveal something essential. Michael Paul was convinced that God's goodness was actively at work in the world and, despite all the messiness of life, he firmly accepted with his fellow-Jesuit and poet Gerard Manley Hopkins that 'the world is charged with the grandeur of God'.

He was a thinker who was open to mystery, like Shakespeare's Hamlet: 'There are more things in heaven and earth, Horatio, than are dreamt of in your philosophy'. Michael Paul naturally gravitated toward thinkers who were alive to intimations of mystery in the familiar and the everyday. He was always on the watch for wonder, reverence and a more marvellous way of seeing things. He did not believe that everything needed to be explained down to the last detail, or presented in a cut-and-dried way. He harboured the hope that God was leading us somewhere we could trust, even though we didn't fully understand where.

He was a self-revealing thinker, and was happy to share his own spiritual experiences. He did not write 'learned' books, with the exception of *Clashing Symbols* which veered in a strongly academic direction. Anyone who has read his other books can testify to the fact that he did not just give reasons and arguments; he also shared himself and who he was.

He was an accessible thinker. Although he was conversant with the thought of difficult and deep theologians, he saw himself as a translator, rephrasing their difficult arguments in a language that could be understood by an educated but non-specialist readership. He peppered his writings with stories from his own experience and quoted liberally from poetry and literature, making his message easier to grasp.

He was an orthodox thinker, but in a compassionate manner. He didn't threaten those who were confused or lost, but reached out to them with kindness and understanding. He had a deep respect for them, wherever they were on the journey of life. He managed to hold together a deep fidelity to the longstanding wisdom of the Church with a true respect for all that was best in the history of thought, whether ancient, medieval or contemporary.

## Imaginative Writer

Michael Paul's style of writing reflected the kind of intellectual he was. It was a style that imaginatively expressed the marvel of life and faith, gathering together the wisdom of great thinkers in a language that touched the heart. Readers – and his students too, of course – loved his knack for blending nuggets of theological wisdom with real-life reflections and his facility for describing the spiritual journey with a personal touch. Since this book is a tribute to his intellectual contribution, I will also try in my own small way to model my writing on his style and approach. In these pages you won't find any footnotes. I'll favour clarity over complexity, and poetic writing over technical jargon. The tone will be middlebrow, not academic.

Michael Paul liked to place inspiring quotations at the beginning of each chapter of his books, the fruit of the wisdom he had harvested. In this book, I'll make that practice mine as well. Except, as you may have already noticed, I'm turning the tables on him, so to speak. I'll start each chapter with a couple of quotations from the man himself.

# INTRODUCTION

# WAVELENGTHS AND CROSSROADS

I stand at a daily crossroads, caught between two conflicting images. One is of holding my life, defensively and alone, in my own hands – the illusion of self-mastery. But another possibility enters if my imagination opens, suddenly or slowly, to a pledge of companionship. Here relationship replaces self-will. The initiative is no longer mine but Another's. *Faith Maps*

Belief in the Resurrection involves more than a unique physical event. It needs a wavelength of the heart, not just an objective inquiry of the data. We love best when we know ourselves loved. And the Resurrection of Jesus is God's love-pledge to us. It opens a totally different perspective on life and death. It is the ultimate sign that God is always a God of life and always an enemy of death. It offers an explosive new image of who we are and where we are going. *Into Extra Time*

*G*rowing up in the small village of Collooney, County Sligo, in the 1940s, Michael Paul experienced wonder as he tuned the wireless in the sitting room. There was something quietly mysterious about turning the knob and watching the arrow silently slide along the illuminated panel with its display of numbered wavelengths. Then, after a few moments of hissing and crackling, there was the sudden joy of hearing crystal-clear sound.

## The Wavelengths of Life

This charming story of the old wireless is a helpful parable as our book begins. Thanks to the spirituality of St Ignatius Loyola, Michael Paul learned to tune in to the deeper wavelength of his own life and to live out of that profound listening. We all experience an ebb and flow of conflicting moods within. Often we're unaware of this flux, but if this conflict of moods comes to our awareness, we have the opportunity to learn from the contrasting wavelengths. The moods that are most audible are the negative ones with their hissing and crackling: doubts, fears, restlessness, anxiety and the feeling of being cut off from others. When we get stuck in the discordance and dissatisfaction these moods bring, we've hit what Ignatius calls desolation. On the other hand, when we get in touch with our positive moods – serenity, joy, feeling enlivened and connected with others – we have reached the crystal-clear wavelength that Ignatius calls consolation. I will have more to say about these contrasting moods later in this book. Suffice it to say for now that Michael Paul learned to live his life out of consolation. Like Ignatius himself, he was convinced that consolation is our default state, our natural condition. This doesn't mean being on a permanent high, but it does mean that the current of our life leads us outwards toward goodness, trust and compassion.

Way back in 1974, when addressing the gathered delegates of the Thirty-Second General Congregation in Rome, Pope Paul VI affirmed the unique Jesuit talent for negotiating difficult thresholds. 'Wherever in the Church,' he said, 'even in the most difficult and extreme fields, at the crossroads of ideologies, in the social trenches, there has been and there is confrontation between the burning exigencies of the human being and the perennial message of the Gospel, here also there have been, and there are, Jesuits.' When we find ourselves at decisive crossroads, many conflicting feelings surge: excitement and anticipation on the one hand, and fear and confusion on the other. Precisely because he was in touch with the inner struggle between consolation and desolation in his own life, Michael Paul was also attuned to the hidden battle of moods in the people he met, as well as to the contrasting signs of hope and hopelessness in the culture around him. So he combined keen self-knowledge, insight into other people and a perceptive analysis of the world in which we live.

## Fresh Discoveries

The following chapters will deal with some of the more significant crossroads Michael Paul encountered during his life. Chapter One will describe the caring, stable background in which he grew up and his early exposure to the new and radical thinking that was emerging elsewhere. Covering some forty years of his life, this may seem a long period to traverse in a single chapter, but not if we remember that the focus is on the development of his thought. His thinking progressed and deepened as he moved from the simplicity of a Sligo childhood to the intellectual stimulation of University College Dublin, and to further studies in Caen, Oxford, Johns Hopkins and beyond. He saw the importance of beginning to think deeply about faith as he encountered the challenge of atheism first-hand. The spirituality he learned at the school of St Ignatius provided him with new ways of thinking as well, and the key Ignatian skill of discernment enabled him to approach intellectual problems with a practical wisdom that never fostered divisiveness but always searched for signs of hope. A year in India and another in Latin America pushed him to reflect systematically on the shallowness of Western culture.

Chapter Two deals with the question of unbelief. In 1965, Pope Paul VI formally entrusted the Jesuits with the mission of tackling atheism. Michael Paul – a real admirer of this pontiff, sometimes called the 'forgotten Pope' – took on Paul VI's charge with huge enthusiasm. Given his exceptional intelligence, it might be expected that he would set about working out new proofs for the existence of God, or at the very least presenting the traditional arguments for God's existence in a fresh way. In fact, he did neither. Instead, true to what he had learned at the school of St Ignatius, Michael Paul focused on the level of *personal disposition*, because he was convinced that it was there the real issue lay.

He started from within, inviting people who had problems with believing to get in touch first with the movements of their inner selves. It's only when we are in touch with our real selves that there is any chance that God can become real for us. Going back to the parable of the wireless, if we approach the question of God in a heady way, we'll only arrive at the crackling wavelength of a first cause or first explanation of the universe. But faith is something fuller and richer than that. It is not knowing about God's existence, but recognising the One who loves us, and that means arriving at the wavelength of wonder. The question of God is a truth of relationship rather than an objective truth. And if we cannot tune in to an open and receptive wavelength within ourselves, we will block our way to God, even if we don't realise the fact.

Chapter Three turns to the question of culture in Michael Paul's thought. He was fond of certain words that already evoke personal and cultural shifts, words such as wavelengths, frontiers, convergences, thresholds and crossroads. These words speak of movement, growth, discovery, attunement, encounter and common ground. Michael Paul's life unfolded in such a way that he found himself constantly at various crossroads: between life and learning, between academic publications and pastoral work, between literature and theology, between faith and unbelief, between reason and the imagination, between contemplation and action, between deep spiritual experiences and seriously intelligent reflection, between high-powered thinkers and non-specialist readers, and – later on – between his location in

18

Rome and living globally. In his final illness, he found himself at the defining threshold between life and death. Because of these various crossroads, he faced a lot of changes in his life, but he didn't bemoan them. On the contrary, he was always enthused by the possibilities for growth and freedom that were present as one way of life gave way to another. He looked out for the hidden gift in every change. He resonated with those simple yet marvellous words of Saint Thérèse of Lisieux that he so liked so much, 'Everything is grace'.

In the chapter on culture, we'll also see how Michael Paul's rich understanding of culture was rooted in what he had learned from St Ignatius about consolation and desolation. Because Michael Paul approached culture with a discerning heart, he never pushed his readers toward the desolation of panic or fear, even in the face of the objectionable features of society. He was saddened at evil, but he wasn't too shocked, because he expected to see the struggles of his own heart reflected in some way in the cultural battles around him. He didn't fall into the temptation of thinking that he himself was perfect and that the whole problem was to be found in the world around him. The self-knowledge he had learned as a Jesuit kept him grounded. 'What is it to be a Jesuit?' asked the fathers of the Thirty-Second General Congregation. 'It is to know that one is a sinner,' was their reply, 'yet called to be a companion of Jesus as Ignatius was'. Although Michael Paul was shrewd enough to see that there were serious problems in the world, he felt it wasn't his place to be its judge. He took his cue from the wise farmer in the gospel story who tells his farmworkers not to pull up the noxious weeds, because there is the danger that in the process they might pull up the good wheat as well (*Mt 13:29*). Instead, the farmer urges them to be patient and to allow both the wheat and the weeds to remain until harvest time.

In Chapter Four we'll mainly look at a poem by Seamus Heaney, which captured for Michael Paul the huge shift from the faith and culture of his childhood to that of today. It's also worth noting that a major part of Michael Paul's own appeal as a thinker lay in his gift for language, and in his poetic way of expressing himself. Some people can write well but are poor speakers. Michael Paul wrote well, but he also had a powerful public presence, speaking fluently in rich, warm bass tones. He was capable of coining evocative phrases, such as 'Church atheist' to denote an unbeliever who rejects the Church yet still believes in God. Moreover, he had a lifelong weakness for alliteration! For instance, in the address he gave on receiving an honorary doctorate at Toronto's Regis College, in November 2012, Michael Paul listed five things he wanted to discuss: Roots, Rationality, Revelation, Rupture and Rapture. He chose the letter 'R' because he was speaking at *Regis* College!

Chapter Five delves into the sense of wonder in Michael Paul's thought. The way that Michael Paul surveyed the many crossroads of his life enabled him to arrive at intellectual and spiritual places that have eluded many other intellectuals. It's the kind of task that the Church expects of Jesuits. As Pope Benedict XVI said to the Jesuits gathered for the Thirty-Fifth General Congregation in February 2008, 'The Church needs you, relies on you and continues to turn to you with trust, particularly to reach those physical and spiritual places which others do not reach or have difficulty in reaching'. Michael Paul's journeying brought him especially to new imaginative spaces. He was encouraged to do so by the precept of St Ignatius to search for God in all things. His conviction was that God was already active and at work in all human hearts. In our chapter on wonder, we'll see how Michael Paul helped many people to reach the gateway to wonder in their own lives. He believed that God was present within them, and so he was confident that an amazing journey of faith could unfold if only they could get in touch with the deepest level of themselves. Because of his conviction about God's presence in people, he looked at them with the kind of attention that conveyed a deep reverence.

Chapter Six surveys the role of the imagination in Michael Paul's *oeuvre*. As we have seen, his understanding of the imagination was rooted in the spirituality of St Ignatius and the place the imagination held in his life and prayer. The story is well known of how Ignatius was struck by a cannonball in combat, shattering his right leg, and endangering his life. As he lay on his bed recuperating, two sets of images played in Ignatius's mind. Sometimes, he would dream of being a flashy courtier and winning the hand of a famous noblewoman. At other times, he would picture himself emulating holy men such as St Francis of Assisi and St Dominic. These images ran and reran in his mind. The first set of images brought him little more than a passing thrill, and they also imprisoned him in the jaded ways of the past. The second set of images gave him a joy that stayed, and also opened up a new sense of himself and of who he could be. Ignatius had become aware of the inner struggle between his true self and his and false self. We'll see that Michael Paul thought of the imagination in a similar way, as something that gives us joy and life, opening up new possibilities for living.

Finally, in Chapter Seven, we go into the question of freedom. Again, there is a strong Ignatian root to Michael Paul's interest in freedom. His daily practice of reflecting on his experience in a prayerful way helped him to grow in self-knowledge, to be purified and to get more and more in touch with the still point at the centre of his being. This regular Ignatian habit of examining his consciousness in a graced way helped him to connect with what he really wanted, with his long-term goals and with his deepest hungers. It was an exercise in freedom, the freedom to love.

*Responses of Love*

Ultimately, it's all about loving, and so it is appropriate to say a few words about three ways in which Michael Paul lovingly responded throughout his life to the spiritual lethargy and loss of purpose he found around him. There is a long Christian tradition of dividing love into two basic categories, the corporal and the spiritual works of mercy. Michael Paul certainly practised the corporal works of mercy, and we'll come across specific examples in these pages of how he fed the hungry and visited the sick and the imprisoned. But since the focus of this book is on his intellectual legacy, it is inevitable that the spiritual works of mercy will stand out more clearly in his life.

In his life and writings, Michael Paul found ways of helping people with their emotional and spiritual needs. These kinds of needs often aren't visible, and are frequently hidden beneath a surface of success and self-confidence. Because he was shaped by St Ignatius's passion for 'helping souls', Michael Paul developed antennae that were alert to these hidden needs. Three of the spiritual works of mercy stand out in particular in Michael Paul's life: instructing the ignorant, counselling the doubtful and comforting the afflicted. It is worth pausing briefly on each one of them here, so that you may find echoes of them in the course of this book, as the story of his life unfolds.

First of all, and perhaps most obviously, Michael Paul was an outstanding teacher and educator. He was also a luminous writer. With his creative angle and his gentle yet challenging style, he helped readers to stop and think again about themselves and their lives. His long years as a lecturer, first at a secular and then at a religious university, put him in contact with numerous young people. He knew how to speak to them in ways that made sense. He translated this efficacy into his written work. He had a sense of how important – and delicate – this vocation of teaching was, both in its oral and written forms. He put his heart into this calling. He was generous in sharing his learning and insights with others, not only in his writings and speeches, but also in the many personal conversations that marked his life and absorbed so much of his time.

As well as his role as teacher, Michael Paul developed powerful skills as a counsellor to the young. He encountered many young people who had little self-confidence, who were unclear about their real identity and undecided about what to do in life. Many of them were anxious and full of doubts, fearful of others, worried about the future and what might happen to them. When going through that awkward phase of life, having someone trustworthy to turn to is like receiving direct help from heaven. For many people, Michael Paul was the angel who helped them during these difficult moments. He was quick to pick up signs of discouragement and despair in those around him, and just as quick to lead them to hope. He was an exceptional mentor. His advice was always tactful. He didn't impose his own agenda on others, but sought to help them see for themselves what the best course was. He was an excellent listener, accustomed to asking God's help before giving advice. In this way, he spoke not only from his intelligence but from a spiritual depth.

Reflecting on all these conversations over the years prompted Michael Paul to ask what was really happening to people in the newly emerging culture of our day. He realised that a new generation was growing up with fewer roots, yet bigger pressures, making it more difficult for them to arrive at a steady level of commitment in their lives. Doubt was easier for many of them; faith was more difficult. By reflecting on these conversations, Michael Paul learned how to distil the essence of what he learned and to organise his thoughts in his writings, hoping to reach a wider audience of searchers whom he would never meet face to face.

The ministry of Jesuits has been described as the ministry of consolation, and so it's not surprising that this was a characteristic of Michael Paul's ministry too. Addressing another General Congregation of Jesuits in October 2016, Pope Francis reminded them that the real work of the Society of Jesus is to offer consolation to God's people, to console everyone so that 'the enemy of human nature does not take away our joy'. Michael Paul was compassionate, and knew that everyone he met, at some point or another, would be fighting a great interior battle. He knew that no one is exempt from suffering, and that in those dark moments everyone wants to be comforted. He was a minister of consolation. He encouraged the discouraged. Many people found the right path because Michael Paul reached out to them.

As a spiritual son of St Ignatius, he learned the golden rule of never making a decision in times of darkness, but always to wait patiently for the dawn. Thanks to that gem of spiritual wisdom, Michael Paul saved many people from making disastrous life-damaging decisions in moments of anxiety or crisis. Even when he developed cancer, he resisted the temptation – though he felt it intensely at times – to withdraw into himself. Instead, he set about writing a diary of his illness that he hoped would help others, shining some spiritual light for them in their own moments of struggle.

Much more will be said about all of these topics later. But now it's time to step back into Michael Paul's early life, and travel to the little village where he grew up.

# CHAPTER ONE
# THE FIRST FORTY YEARS

I myself grew up in a smallish village in the West of Ireland in the forties and fifties – before the arrival of so-called modernity. So my roots were traditional and rural. Being thrown into the totally different horizon of university pushed me to ponder what on earth was happening to people in the new culture of today. ***Where is your God?***

Over years, what I might call my pastoral credo has emerged: people are hungry for a different space of self-hearing and self-healing, and when they find it they spontaneously start looking for God. In the experience of human presence and relationship we glimpse the gateway into a mystery that surrounds us – that we live and move within another Presence and are invited into another Relationship. ***Dive Deeper***

*A*round the turn of the millennium, some forty years after he had left it, Michael Paul revisited the place where he had grown up, Collooney in Co. Sligo. He was showing some Italian friends around Ireland, and they had asked to see the village of his childhood. He brought them into what had been the sitting room of his house, and bought a bar of chocolate. This section of his house was now a little supermarket. Where the family had listened to the wireless decades before, a cash register now stood. He didn't know the owners; in fact, he had no relations in the entire village any more. Together with his Italian friends, he walked down the main street of Collooney, and was able to remember every house and the people who lived there in the 1940s and 1950s. They went into the church where he had served as an altar boy. Everything was as alive for him as though it were yesterday; and yet yesterday seemed like another world. A little later he did bump into some people who recognised him, and they warmly welcomed him home; but he knew well that this place was no longer home.

That trip down memory lane captured for Michael Paul the contrast between where he came from and the world into which he had arrived. The village of Collooney was a small world and a complete world. It provided him with a whole nourishing menu for the spirit and the imagination. It gave him deep roots which were a continual blessing, even if he was largely unaware of this blessing from day to day. It shaped the way he felt about things, and the way he pictured and imagined reality. Later he learned to live in more complex worlds, of course. Now, as he strolled through his native village conversing in Italian, he became aware of this massive shift of horizons. Together with his friends he visited his former schoolroom, where once there had been a turf fire in the corner which the frequent downpours would put out. As a child, he had studied Irish, English, History and Geography in this room. Now, he could recall the many places he had visited that then had been mere names on the rotating globe: India, Venezuela, Kenya, Ethiopia, Australia, New Zealand, Iran, Malaysia, Vietnam. As for his former school, it had been converted into a cattle shed.

As we look at the first forty years of Michael Paul's life, we will see how he first became exposed to a new and complex world, and how he discovered that he had a unique gift for making sense of faith in this challenging environment. Born in 1939, there was nothing in his typically Irish childhood to indicate that this new world was on the way. The culture of his childhood village was simple and unified. He liked to quote a line from a poem of Wallace Stevens that expresses well this all-encompassing and complete world: 'We were as Danes in Denmark all day long'. Both his parents were doctors, and Michael Paul himself was their only child. When he was twelve years of age, his parents sent him to Clongowes Wood College, the Jesuit boarding school in Co. Kildare. Although he wasn't much good at sports, he was academically gifted and was outstanding in drama and debating. In terms of his faith, he later thought of his young self as rather pious.

After school, he studied for three years at University College Dublin. During his university studies, he lived in Nullamore, the Opus Dei hostel in Dublin, where he was encouraged to reflect upon his faith in a more active way. He went to Mass frequently, though not every day, and began to nourish his faith intellectually by reading theology, and spiritually by using Scripture as a foundation for prayer. He didn't experience Catholicism as narrow or oppressive in those days, though in retrospect he did see that it had been passive and somewhat insulated from reality.

## The French Connection

Just after he finished his degree in English and French literature, Michael Paul received a grant from the French State to study in Caen for a year. For him, it was a wonderful year of expanding horizons and new discoveries. He moved from the sheltered world of Irish Catholicism to the diverse and complex atmosphere of French Catholicism. For the first time in his life he met significant numbers of agnostics as well as Catholics who were distanced from their faith. But the biggest surprise of all was encountering French Catholics who were passionate about their faith. They met together to read the Bible, they went to pray in local monasteries, they organised talks about social issues, and they invited well-known thinkers, such as Gabriel Marcel, to speak to them.

What really made him reflect in a new way was the initially

bewildering blend of two different worlds. On the one hand, he found a thoughtful, engaged and dynamic Catholicism. This compelling face of Christianity helped him find new depth in his own faith. Slowly he began to realise that the Incarnation meant that God truly loved the world and embraced human reality in all its strengths and weaknesses. It dawned on him that everyday life had also become sacred, thanks to Jesus making it his own, and that spiritual growth wasn't just something that happened in rarefied moments of contemplation, but could also blossom amidst the humdrum routine of ordinary life.

On the other hand, he was surprised to discover that many of his fellow students had deserted the Church, and even religion, altogether. Engaging in lengthy conversations with many of these, often into the early hours of the morning, Michael Paul learned something valuable that would stand the test of time. He came to see that he had the gift of shifting conversations about faith from an argumentative tone to one of open and personal searching. This gift for moving people from the head to the heart stayed with him throughout his life. In fact, he became better at it, so much so that it became second nature to him. He deftly moved his conversation partners from cerebral arguments to inner exploration before they even noticed that he had done so.

He used this gift in his writings as well. Although he wrote again and again about faith and unbelief, it is telling that he hardly ever invoked the traditional arguments for God's existence. That is because he felt it was vital to let go of cleverness in order to enter into a deeper kind of questioning. By themselves, he knew that arguments can be counterproductive. It is only when we are standing on the wave of wonder that we can begin to sail toward God in a satisfying way. Later, when he gave talks and lectures around the world, he used his talent for deepening the agenda again and again when confronted with seemingly awkward theoretical questions. With surprising ease, he was able to plunge questioners into a deeper level of life and of themselves.

Linked with this liberating method of engaging with people, the year in France also witnessed the birth of his big intellectual passion, a passion that grew and sharpened in the years that followed. This was the desire to make God meaningful for the people around him, above all for unbelievers.

There was also a human passion that burst into life during that year in Caen. Michael Paul met a shy, tender and loving young woman called Monique. Afterwards, he hardly ever spoke of her. Although he knew Monique for only a brief period, the impact of that relationship lasted a lifetime. This is shown by the fact that he deliberately chose to close his final and posthumously published book, *Into Extra Time*, with a poem commemorating her. The unforgettable memory of Monique is his last testament to his readers. He entitled the poem, 'Monique in Caen'.

> The heart carries more than memories:
> When I think of you, of us, or see a photo,
> All is alive like yesterday.
> I wonder what happened to you,
> what you did with that tenderness,
> With the shy strength of your gaze.
> Did the years harden or soften your beauty?
> Did you forget me, hurt by my silence
> Let down by my different path? Or can you visit,
> as I do, wonder echoes
> Of hands held and eyes knit,
> Symbols of a love bigger than
> we were able for at twenty one,
> but changing me at least forever.

## Jesuit Novitiate

After returning from his exhilarating year in Caen, Michael Paul joined the Jesuits on 8 October 1961. He had been toying with the idea of a Jesuit vocation for a number of years, even before he finished secondary school. Had he joined immediately after his Leaving Cert, he might have been entering religious life with a somewhat suspicious stance toward the world. France had changed all that in a decisive manner, however. He now had a big vision for his life, the desire to make sense of faith for unbelievers. The world of unbelief was no longer a world he feared, because he had encountered so many young French people who were struggling with faith, and many of them were now his friends.

Michael Paul's novitiate was in Emo, Co. Laois. His novice master was Fr Patrick Cusack SJ, a man with a special gift for teaching people how to pray. In truth, Fr Cusack emphasised that he himself couldn't teach people how to pray; only God could do that. But Fr Cusack managed to demystify prayer for his novices, showing them that it was essentially quite simple, a matter of talking to God in a straightforward and unaffected way. Prayer, for him, was similar to a child talking to a loving parent. And, like a child who is sure of the love of a father or mother, so too, if we know we are loved by God, we can allow ourselves to be who we are when we come before him in prayer. Fr Cusack encouraged his novices to develop the habit of praying; not just to think about prayer, but to do it. He emphasised that they would only learn how to pray by praying regularly, and by making prayer part of their lives.

Soon after beginning his novitiate, Michael Paul, along with his fellow novices, spent thirty days making the Spiritual Exercises in total silence. Following the pattern suggested by St Ignatius Loyola in a book of the same name from the sixteenth century, this experience of prayer is the cornerstone of Ignatian spirituality. It is one of those seminal books that has touched the lives of millions of Christians. In the words of Pope Paul VI, 'The practice of the Exercises constitutes not only an invigorating and restorative breather for the spirit in the midst of the noise of modern life, but even more so today an irreplaceable school to introduce souls to greater intimacy with God, to the love of virtue and to the true knowledge of life, as a gift of God and as a response to his call'. The Spiritual Exercises are designed to lead the retreatant into a deeper relationship with God and also a greater sense of purpose in life. Ignatius always expected union with God to bear fruit in concrete reality; any new intimacy with God inevitably throws light on the decisive choices to be made in life. So, for Ignatius, a double dimension is always present: encountering God in prayer and forming our life's choices in a newly graced way as a result.

Ignatius got in touch with his deepest experiences of God and named these experiences for what they were. As well as the positive experiences, Ignatius acknowledged the sinful ones as well. The stamp of personal experience gives his spirituality tremendous power: what's most personal is most universal. Through the Spiritual Exercises, others are opened up to a deep experience of God as they go through this structured journey of prayer and meditation.

We can get some idea of how Ignatian spirituality touched Michael Paul, both then and throughout his life, from this imaginary letter that he wrote to St Ignatius on 31 July 2015, the saint's feast day. As it turned out, this was to be the last opportunity he would have to celebrate the feast day of the founder of the Jesuits.

Dear Ignatius,
On your feast day for 2015 I want to thank you for the lights you have given me down through the years. When I was younger perhaps the key discovery that you passed on to me

was to recognise my pendulum of movements or moods, what you called consolation and desolation. Here was a space of ordinary revelation. Linked to this was the golden rule never to make a decision in the dark, but to wait for dawn. This has become a nugget of spiritual wisdom for many people I have known.

A related insight was to see God in all things, at work in the theatre of the ordinary. You insisted that we should reflect back prayerfully on the day we have lived and therefore develop antennae, alert to the invitations of the Good Spirit (and to our receiving them or running away). In this way you encouraged us to be spiritual but not too much so, not withdrawn from the human. You were to be found within the human adventure of each day and indeed within each chapter of history.

A third influence you had on me was your passion for 'helping souls'. The school of prayer in your *Spiritual Exercises* aimed at liberating us to serve Christ's Kingdom and to give of ourselves to people. I also learned that urgency of mission can take many forms. Look at the diversity of ministry and of personality among us Jesuits!

In later years I began to appreciate more your mystical side. In the *Exercises* you spoke of God's 'immediate work' as 'embracing us in love'. Simply to rest in that love becomes a deeper call as life goes on, just as the love-presence of the Trinity became a source of powerful devotion for you (so often overwhelmed by tears). You probably never saw Rublev's famous icon. For me the fourth place at that table captures the extraordinary call to enter the flow of love that is our triune God.

So thank you for having guided my lifelong and changing

adventure of freedom in the Lord. Not for nothing did you put freedom first among the gifts you wanted to offer back to God: Take and receive, O Lord, my freedom.

Happy feast, dear Pilgrim.

## *Poetry at Oxford*

When he had completed his two years of novitiate, Michael Paul went to Oxford in the autumn of 1963 to study the English literature of the Renaissance. There he wrote a thesis on the theme of rhetoric in the poetry of George Herbert. This Anglican priest, who died of consumption at the age of thirty-nine in 1633, became Michael Paul's favourite poet from that time onwards. Michael Paul loved the exceptional spiritual purity of Herbert's poems, and he warmed to his character as well, a man blessed with great brilliance and extraordinary humility. As a seventeen-year-old beginning his studies at the University of Cambridge, Herbert wrote to his mother in words that are reminiscent of the Latin motto of the Jesuits, *ad majorem Dei gloriam*. Herbert promised 'that my poor abilities in poetry shall be all and ever consecrated to God's glory'.

Herbert was true to his word. In fact, he was so shy and humble about his poems that on his deathbed he had them sent to his friend Nicholas Ferrar, leaving it up to Ferrar to decide whether they should be published or burned. 'Tell him', he wrote, 'he shall find in it a picture of the many spiritual conflicts that have passed betwixt God and my soul, before I could subject mine to the will of Jesus my Master; in whose service I have now found perfect freedom'.

Michael Paul found inspiration in 'the many spiritual conflicts that have passed betwixt God and my soul', in the honesty with which Herbert portrayed his spiritual ups and downs, and in the ebb and flow between light and darkness. He also noted that, despite these fluctuations, Herbert never lost hope; in spite of feeling dried out by life at times, a new blossoming was always possible. The poem 'The Flower' expresses well this sense of astonishment at new beginnings:

> Who would have thought my shrivelled heart
> Could have recovered greenness?

Herbert's depiction of the conflict between light and darkness touched a chord within Michael Paul. He also admired the ultimately hopeful tone of Herbert's poems; for Herbert, God's grace always breaks through our human fragility. Michael Paul also learned from this master of language – Herbert was elected Public Orator at Cambridge, had exemplary Latin, and in addition was a gifted musician – about the importance of the words we use to speak about spiritual things. For instance, the effect of the poem 'Love III', which the brilliant Jewish mystic Simone Weil (1909–43) called the most beautiful poem ever written, is much more powerful because Herbert uses the word 'Love' instead of 'God'.

> Love bade me welcome. Yet my soul drew back
>> Guilty of dust and sin.
> But quick-eyed Love, observing me grow slack
>> From my first entrance in,
> Drew nearer to me, sweetly questioning
>> If I lacked anything.

This poem, like most of Herbert's poems, is deceptively simple. Love is portrayed as overwhelmingly polite, totally non-calculating, relentless in generosity, thoroughly irresistible, and completely undeserved on the part of the recipient.

> 'A guest,' I answered, 'worthy to be here':
> Love said, 'You shall be he.'

'I, the unkind, ungrateful? Ah, my dear,
     I cannot look on thee.'
Love took my hand, and smiling did reply,
     'Who made the eyes but I?'

The conversation continues in the next and final stanza, with the guest still hesitant and Love yet more persistent:

'Truth, Lord, but I have marred them: let my shame
     Go where it doth deserve.'
'And know you not', says Love, 'who bore the blame?'
     'My dear, then I will serve.'
'You must sit down,' says Love, 'and taste my meat.'
     So I did sit and eat.

It is worth noting that in this powerful poem, Love never becomes something that can be grasped; it always remains mysterious. In the course of the poem Love becomes thoroughly appealing and approachable, however, because of the delicacy, tact and generosity shown to the speaker. While only hesitatingly grateful at the start of the poem, by the end the speaker is utterly amazed. Michael Paul learned to use language with a skill that echoed Herbert's: with care, creativity and craft.

Michael Paul's thesis on the poetry of George Herbert was supervised by Professor Helen Gardner. Dame Helen Gardner was one of the leading lights in English Studies at the time, an extremely bright, elegant and forthright woman, and an excellent teacher. She had a kindness to her that she didn't broadcast to the world. For instance, unknown to C. S. Lewis, she withdrew her application for a fellowship in Cambridge mainly because she heard that Lewis had decided he was interested. Helen Gardner was an acknowledged authority on the poetry of John Donne, George Herbert and T. S. Eliot. One of the abiding themes of interest for Michael Paul – the imagination – was also a deep source of interest for her. In fact, a couple of decades later she was to publish a book entitled *In Defence of the Imagination* (1982). Helen Gardner regarded the imagination as the human power that helps us to break out of the narrow limits of ourselves, freeing us to enter into the lives of others and freeing us, in a sense, to become another person. That generous and resilient view of the imagination must have resonated with her young Jesuit graduate student from Ireland.

At Oxford, Michael Paul again encountered many unbelievers among his fellow students. He wondered how he could find a language to get through to them. He needn't have worried: the answer came from none other than George Herbert himself. After a number of seminars on the poetry of Herbert, it dawned on Michael Paul that this Welsh-born poet's marvellous manner of expressing the inner life made sense to everyone, whether believer or unbeliever. Whereas overtly religious language easily put people off, the language of literature moved them deeply. England crowned the intuitions to which his year in France had given birth. France had given him the passion to explore unbelief, not by using the dry language of doctrine, but by using the imaginative vocabulary of poetry, drama and novels. His literary studies in England richly confirmed this intuitive approach.

### Philosophy

From 1965 to 1967 Michael Paul studied philosophy at Heythrop College, which at that time was located near the village of Chipping Norton in West Oxfordshire. The very year he began his studies of philosophy, Pope Paul VI gave a historic speech to a group of Jesuit leaders and delegates gathered for a decisive meeting in Rome, the Thirty-First General Congregation of the Society of Jesus.

On that occasion, Pope Paul VI asked the Jesuits to tackle atheism in a systematic, rigorous and even saintly way. He specifically entrusted Jesuits with the mission 'of making a stout, united stand against atheism … to do research, to gather information of all kinds, to publish material, to hold discussions among themselves, to prepare specialists in the field, to pray, to be shining examples of justice and holiness, skilled and well-versed in an eloquence of word and example made bright by heavenly grace'. The worldwide spread of atheism since 1965 is clear evidence of how prophetic Pope Paul VI's call was. Atheism has indeed grown and spread, and it shows no signs of going away. This means that the mission Paul VI entrusted to the Society of Jesus will inevitably be a long-term one.

These words of Pope Paul VI were also a confirmation of Michael Paul's own burgeoning interest in the question of unbelief. Michael Paul had to figure out how exactly to make a 'stand against atheism' and how to apply 'an eloquence of word and example' to this new mission, one of the most momentous charges ever entrusted by a pope to the Society of Jesus. By nature Michael Paul wasn't a hard-nosed person and, as we have seen, he preferred dialogue to confrontation as the way forward. Happily, his own personal style was suited to engaging fruitfully with the new forms of atheism that were emerging.

In the traditional approach to atheism, Catholic apologists would have been inclined to argue that atheism was erroneous for certain reasons, and they would have then listed and explained these reasons in logical order. That approach made a lot of sense in addressing atheistic theories which had an identifiable content and structure, such as those originating in Marxist philosophy and in Communist ideologies. But the kind of atheism that was beginning to take hold in the 1960s was largely due to the new materialistic outlook in the affluent West and the steady drift away from Christianity in previously staunch Christian nations such as France.

In addition, the unthinking acceptance of science as the only valid explanation of the world – the notion that the only things that are true are those that we can observe and physically measure – was eroding many people's openness to God and the transcendent. So it was not only a matter of understanding what was inadequate or wrong with atheism, but also of trying to work out why people were being drawn to it. And that meant going beyond logical arguments to explore the impact of ways of living and world views. If the atheism most current in our world was not for the most part a worked-out doctrine, rebutting it on logical grounds wouldn't be sufficient to stop people adhering to it.

In relation to the challenge of science to faith, Michael Paul benefited from the thoughtful approach of one of his favourite professors at Heythrop College, Fr Thomas Gornall SJ. Gornall was the professor of natural theology and the history of ancient philosophy in the college, and he had published a short and useful book, *A Philosophy of God*, a few years before Michael Paul started studying there. One of Michael Paul's fellow students had just completed a science degree and zealously promoted the scientific way of seeing reality. One day this student spoke at length about the view of the world provided by evolution. Fr Gornall, after listening graciously to this long intervention, gently replied, 'Perhaps you haven't really begun to do philosophy yet. We're asking a different kind of question altogether. You are describing a process. But what we're doing here is trying to explain why everything exists, everything. You have to shift from the "how" question to the "why" question; and this "why" question surpasses science.'

The student wasn't to be quietened so easily, however. 'How would St Thomas Aquinas respond to the challenge of evolution?' he asked. Father Gornall calmly replied, 'The Angelic Doctor would say that evolution, although a fine description, is a woefully inadequate explanation. Is a rose truly nothing more than a collection of atoms?'

It was not only what Gornall said that Michael Paul appreciated, but also how he said it. By his way of replying, this wise professor was urging the self-certain student to let go of his intellectual exhibitionism and to open himself up instead to a deeper kind of questioning. We can speak at length about the world and how it works, but to deliberate in a reflective way about why anything at all exists is quite a different matter. Fr Gornall's tactful way of moving the agenda from description to depth was a technique that Michael Paul himself already practised and would skilfully hone over time. Like Gornall, Michael Paul was able to shift the terms of a discussion from fruitless arguments to fruitful explorations.

## *Lecturing and Further Studies*

From 1967 to 1969 Michael Paul had the opportunity to confirm the correctness of these intuitions through practical experience. In the autumn of 1967 he began lecturing in English literature for a year at University College Dublin. There he got to know several students who would later become well-known writers and film directors. Listening to them and to others like them, Michael Paul felt like he was being projected into the future. He was getting a glimpse of the first signs of a profound cultural shift that was already under way. Several months later, at a gathering of the Irish Jesuits, Michael Paul boldly announced that Irish culture was changing and that faith was no longer something that could be taken for granted. Those Jesuits at the gathering who were not in contact with the new generation were taken aback at the candid opinions of their twenty-eight-year-old confrère.

Later in that summer of 1968, Michael Paul travelled to the USA for a year as a research fellow at Johns Hopkins University in Baltimore. He arrived in a city that had been rocked by riots a couple of months beforehand. Immediately after the assassination of Martin Luther King on 4 April 1968, Baltimore, like other cities across the USA, exploded into a rampage of burning, looting and rock-throwing. The frustration that had been simmering for years in the ghettos suddenly ignited. At the time, Michael Paul wasn't sure how to incorporate this literally burning issue of social justice into his vision of faith, but a number of years later, after he spent time in India and Latin America, his view of faith expanded to embrace the social dimension.

At the Department of English in Johns Hopkins University, Michael Paul ran into a revolt of a different kind, a challenge to the classical view of literature he had learned at Oxford. He was witnessing the first stirrings of what would later become an intellectual fashion in literary studies: postmodernism. Postmodernism involves a kind of thinking that takes things apart instead of building them up, with 'deconstruction' as one of its main tools. Almost thirty years later, Michael Paul would write a book on culture – *Clashing Symbols* – where, true to his tendency to see the elements of good in everything, he was able to list the positive as well as the negative elements in our postmodern culture. He discerned in the midst of many fragmented, drifting and postmodern lifestyles a simultaneous hunger for wholeness, connectedness and mystery.

This gift for seeing surprising opportunities for renewal where others only saw disintegration was characteristic of Michael Paul. Perhaps the most valuable lesson he learned from that year in Maryland was further confirmation of his desire to seek out an imaginative wavelength in his dialogue with unbelievers. In his friendship with agnostic Jewish students at Johns Hopkins, Michael Paul once again found implicit evidence that the imaginative world of literature was much more fertile common ground than long heady arguments could ever be.

*Theology*

Equipped with a rich background in literature, Michael Paul began to study theology at the newly established Milltown Institute in Dublin in the autumn of 1969. This move was inevitably a little underwhelming for him. At thirty years of age, he had sat at the feet of world-famous professors in Oxford and Johns Hopkins, he had interacted with some of the brightest students in France, the UK and the USA, and he had lectured the cream of Ireland's rising creative generation. Now, he was beginning again. In addition, the theology he was taught was too 'churchy' for his liking. The focus of theological studies in those years was primarily on Church concerns: close scrutiny of the Church's teaching on doctrinal and moral issues, a clear understanding of the sacraments and a grasp of Church history. Michael Paul recognised the importance of becoming acquainted with the venerable tradition of theology and its long history. Nevertheless, his experience in France, Britain and the USA had given him a real passion for the concerns of the world outside the Church, for how real people were struggling with their faith. And so he experienced in those years a frustrating gap between what he was required to study in terms of official theology and what he had seen in terms of lived concerns.

While he was studying his undergraduate theology, Michael Paul experienced two saving graces. First, he came to know a learned and holy Jesuit professor, Fr John Hyde SJ, who impressed him not just by his wide erudition but even more by his saintliness. (There will be a little more about this influential man in the last chapter of this book.) Second, Michael Paul was invited to continue lecturing in English at UCD during his theological studies – a most unusual arrangement for a Jesuit in formation. So he spent the mornings as a student in Milltown, and the afternoons or evenings as a lecturer in the English Department at UCD. He enjoyed the challenge of studying theology while also engaging with an ambience that was becoming more secular, observing all the time how the changed atmosphere was affecting students. He was also able to bring his literary background into theology by, for instance, comparing how literary criticism was applied to the Bible and to classic works of English literature.

## Charismatic Renewal

Michael Paul was ordained to the priesthood on 23 June 1972. In the autumn he returned full-time to his post as lecturer in modern English literature, where he remained, with one interruption, for the next eighteen years. A couple of months before he was ordained, Michael Paul attended a Charismatic Renewal prayer meeting in Dublin for the first time. This spiritual movement within the Catholic Church, which promotes a first-hand experience of the power of the Holy Spirit and a personal relationship with Jesus, had spread from the United States to Ireland around that time.

The story of Michael Paul's relationship with the Charismatic Renewal is not one of dramatic change, but of steady growth. He was to experience some privileged moments of grace, but overall the deepening of his spiritual life was gradual, although at the same time thoroughly real. He didn't experience an instantaneous entry into a new sense of God, but he did discover that God, prayer and priestly ministry took on a new reality for him.

Michael Paul's reactions to his first charismatic prayer meeting were mixed. He was attracted by the free-flowing spontaneous prayer and by the upbeat singing of hymns, but he didn't feel comfortable with all the talk about praising God. It took him several months to realise that praise hadn't really been central to his faith, which is why he sometimes struggled with the more exuberant psalms in the Breviary. In a more serious way, he was ill at ease with the apparently exaggerated nature of the faith of some people around him. One evening, after a particularly exuberant meeting, he went home asking if he really believed at all. Despite these reactions, however, he kept going to meetings, alternating between interest and scepticism. Toward the end of 1972 he began to attend a smaller prayer meeting where he felt more at home.

As time went on, Michael Paul began to appreciate more the opportunity to pray aloud with others and to be nourished by their faith and support, but he remained uncomfortable with the more dramatic aspects of these meetings. Nevertheless, over the next couple of years, he found that his faith was deepening significantly through the experience of group worship and through his friendship with individuals. Eventually, he decided to ask for 'baptism in the Holy Spirit', even though he disliked the phrase itself and was uncomfortable with how some people understood it. For Michael Paul, it meant asking others to pray for him that God would enable him to experience his power and presence more fully, and that the graces of baptism and confirmation would be brought alive in new ways for him.

In fact, Michael Paul was certain that he had already experienced a gradual liberation by the Holy Spirit simply by attending these prayer meetings. He recognised several signs of this new-found freedom in himself: he began to pray openly with individuals who came to him for help, instead of merely giving them advice; his way of preaching had become more personal; he was able to help searchers in a more direct way by testifying to how God was working in his own life; and he even prayed quietly in tongues on a few occasions, feeling deep satisfaction that his prayer had gone beyond any words he knew and yet was more expansive than pure silence.

The actual moment of his 'baptism in the Spirit' was quite ordinary and unspectacular. During a Saturday evening prayer meeting, a group of people laid hands on him and prayed over him, while Michael Paul himself expressed his own faith in Jesus and asked that

Jesus become more and more the Lord of his life. Later that night, however, Michael Paul had a surprising spiritual experience. On his way home, he stopped by a church, entering into the dark by a side door. As soon as he was there, he experienced a sudden desire to say the rosary. This was totally unexpected because, apart from public occasions, he had not himself prayed the rosary in recent years. Now he found himself praying with real passion, praising God in a way he had never done before as he uttered the familiar words, 'Glory be to the Father and to the Son and to the Holy Spirit'. He had a powerful sense of Mary's role in guiding him into the fullness of Jesus and of the Spirit. Looking around him, he noticed to his surprise that he was kneeling beside a statue of Our Lady that he hadn't even realised was there. The following morning he prayed the psalms of praise in his breviary with particular gusto. From then on in prayer meetings he exercised the gift of 'prophecy', not by foretelling the future, but by 'forth-telling': speaking to others of God, and offering them a few words to help them sense God's love and closeness.

Although he stopped attending prayer meetings after a few years, the spiritual fruits endured. Michael Paul felt a fresh sense of freedom in his life, his faith, his priesthood and his ministry, a freedom that came from being more deeply rooted in the Spirit and more closely connected with others. He began to appreciate the official Church in a new way, seeing below surface appearances, and in his celebration of Mass he found himself praying for the pope in a heartfelt way. But most of all he sensed new possibilities if he could somehow allow God to work through him instead of trying to do God's work all by himself.

### India: the Challenge of Injustice

In 1976, Michael Paul travelled to India for the final stage of his Jesuit formation, called tertianship. This programme of prayer, experience and reflection is sometimes called the school of the heart, because its focus is indeed on 'heart learning'. As well as making the full Spiritual Exercises for the second time, Michael Paul's tertianship saw him working in leper colonies and helping out in Mother Teresa's home for the dying in the city then known as Calcutta, now Kolkata.

His work in the home for the dying involved all sorts of humble service, from dabbing lotion on the back of a patient with scabies to fetching tea for an elderly man unable to move from his bed. Encountering the extreme needs and suffering of so many people, Michael Paul found himself wondering what it all meant for him. It was one thing to help out in a home for the dying for a short time, but how was he to live his life for others after his return to the West? He found this a difficult question to answer, because it brought him face to face with a deep struggle in his own heart, a struggle between discouragement, guilt and hope. The discouragement came from the sheer scale of the suffering he was seeing: wouldn't anything he did just be an ineffectual drop in the ocean? Fear that he would fail to be the person he wanted to be brought with it a sense of guilt. But he also found a source of hope in himself when he came to accept that the life he was called to was really about surrendering to God's initiative rather than being in control himself.

One warm summer evening, as Michael Paul walked through the streets of Calcutta, he noticed a child lying on the footpath. He assumed that the child was asleep, but afterwards he wondered if he might be sick or even dying. When it came to his own mealtime, Michael Paul was unable to eat, so preoccupied was he with the memory of the child. So he put some of his own food into a bag and retraced his steps. He eventually found the child, fast asleep on the pavement, and shook him gently until he woke up. Although the boy was initially wary of this unknown stranger, he readily ate the food offered him. He didn't speak any English, so after patting him on the head, Michael Paul returned home.

Back in his room, still thinking of the child on the footpath, he prayed. He begged God to do something about the child's situation. After a while, in the stillness, it seemed that he heard an answer in his own heart: 'But I am doing something – I created you'. It was a phrase that Michael Paul had come across in one of Anthony de Mello's stories, but now it had become unexpectedly and distinctly his own.

The following morning Michael Paul got up particularly early, and set out to find the boy and see what more he could do. Arriving at the spot, he discovered that the boy was no longer there; in fact the whole street was empty. Then, on the other side of the street, he noticed a boy picking through a rubbish bin, but when he caught sight of Michael Paul, he disappeared around a corner. Was this the same boy that he had come across the evening before? He would never know, but the image of that boy would never leave him. It was with the help of that image that he would afterwards hear the voice of God reminding him, 'I am doing something – I created you'.

Up until 1976, there had been three notes in Michael Paul's chord of faith. First, the note of belonging: he grew up with a strong sense of belonging to the Church, and during his teenage years, this sense of belonging developed into a personal relationship with Jesus. The second note in his chord of faith was conviction. At college, he did have his doubts, but the faith he had inherited was strong enough to hold together. Even during the year in France, which broadened his horizons, and where his inherited kind of Catholicism appeared unusual and even odd, his core conviction was not undermined. The third note was vocation. It was as a result of his year in France that he felt called to become a Jesuit. The three notes of his chord of faith grew louder and more distinct as time went on. He was faithful to the Church in the deepest part of his being. He practised regular personal prayer throughout his life, nurturing his sense of God and closeness to Jesus. And he relished making the vision of Christ credible and attractive for a new generation.

His six months in India marked the first sounding of a new note in this chord. It was concerned with how the gospel was lived in society, and introduced the note of justice into his chord of faith. It wasn't a matter of abandoning the first three notes, of course. It was more a matter of going beyond any narrowness to which they might have led. Michael Paul's faith began to wake up from an earlier naiveté. He began to see that society exerted a significant influence on people, and this influence could either awaken them to spiritual realities or make them spiritually impoverished.

Michael Paul's background and temperament had made him more at home in dealing with faith than with issues of justice. He loved enabling people to make sense of Christ in a way that was personally real and spiritually authentic. His daily contact with university students meant that he was constantly helping individuals who were labouring to make sense of who they were and of a faith from which many of them had become distanced. Until now, he hadn't had a huge amount of contact with poor people, with the unemployed or with those at the margins of society. India began to change all that.

Working with lepers and the dying in Calcutta, Michael Paul experienced a long slow shudder as he saw that poverty was not something that affected just a few, but a way of life to which most people there were condemned. Things became even clearer when he returned from India. In Ireland, he found anger rising inside himself when he saw the opulence on display at home compared to the poverty of India.

Michael Paul had moved from compassion for the plight of individuals to a more general awareness of how injustice can be systemic, built into the very fabric of society. He was also keenly aware that at an international gathering of leading Jesuits in Rome in 1974

– the Thirty-Fourth General Congregation – the Society of Jesus had committed itself to the promotion of justice as an essential element in the service of faith. Not all Jesuits were clear what this new principle would look like in practice, especially as it applied to traditional works of the Society, such as education. Whatever it meant concretely, all Jesuits realised, as Michael Paul did, that they had to connect their existing view of faith with this new sense of justice.

## Integrating Faith and Justice

Michael Paul was gentle with others, but he could be sometimes hard on himself, feeling that he should be doing more. Especially in the area of justice, he needed to apply all his skills of discernment in order not to fall into the temptation of doing too much, and of trying to live more than one life at a time. It was sometimes a real effort for him to stay anchored in serenity and joy, and not to get caught into a cycle of blame and self-guilt. The following story illustrates this inner struggle, and the victory of a sense of peace over the impulse toward dissatisfaction.

He once gave a short talk on the radio where he spoke about the demanding task of living at various crossroads in life. He spoke of visiting a friend in prison. His friend had just been sent to jail after a hurried trial at which Michael Paul was not allowed to speak in his defence. His friend was still coming to terms with being incarcerated. He was barely eating, and wasn't sleeping at all. They spoke for the full half hour that was allowed. Michael Paul left the prison with all sorts of sad images in his mind – the silent row of young faces, the dinner trays brought to solitary cells, the drained look of his friend. As he walked down the street, he felt haunted by these desolate images.

An hour later, Michael Paul found himself in a completely different place. He was in a university library, surrounded by the young faces of students anxiously cramming before exams. As he was doing his research, he suddenly found the images from the prison returning in force. The library was barely a mile away from the prison, yet it was another world.

He wondered if he could make a bridge between these two different worlds. Was his life just a disconnected series of fragments that were impossible to put together? He knew that his imprisoned friend would probably never find himself in a university library. Could there be any true link between these so very different worlds, the prison and the library? He knew that if there was to be a link, if would have to come from something bigger than himself.

As he sat in the bus on the way home, he opened the New Testament, and his eyes were drawn by the phrase, 'In him all things hold together' (*Col 1:17*). That's when it hit him. It dawned upon him that Jesus is the one who brings together the prison and the library, if only he could stay open to him and allow him to do so. He knew that Jesus himself would have been more likely to visit a prison than a library, but he also knew that at this particular moment Jesus was inviting Michael Paul to do both. He was urging him to read books in a way that would be true to his friend in prison. In fact, Jesus was challenging him to do everything in harmony with Jesus' compassion for the world, the only power that can glue all the pieces together.

Interestingly, in the two decades following the new Jesuit emphasis on working for justice, more and more Jesuits began to see that justice and culture were thoroughly bound up with each other. As a result, at a subsequent worldwide Jesuit assembly in 1995 – the Thirty-Fourth General Congregation – justice was inserted into the wider framework of culture and dialogue. This global gathering of Jesuits gave official backing to an intuition that had been growing in Michael Paul over the years: the importance of culture. Michael Paul had already begun to see how we are shaped – and sometimes misshaped – by the ways of life of the societies in which we find ourselves.

But I'll press the pause button now, because I'm in danger of running ahead of myself. In fact, before Michael Paul explored the crucial role that culture plays in forming our values and vision, he spent several years studying atheism and unbelief in depth. It was because of his study of atheism that he began to realise how decisive a role culture plays in our lives. In the next chapter, we'll turn to the question of unbelief.

But before we do so, it is important to say a few words about an important service he provided for hundreds of young Jesuits, helping to form them into human and spiritual maturity.

## Formation of Young Jesuits

Michael Paul played a crucial role in the formation of many young Jesuits, both in Ireland and Rome. He brought to this role his own rich and varied experience as a Jesuit. That made a big difference, because he wasn't simply forming young men for some vague ministry in the future. He was helping them to become full members of the Society of Jesus at a time of change, serving people in a specifically Jesuit way and using the particular gifts they possessed.

For various reasons, it wasn't an easy role for Michael Paul. It meant, for instance, that every feature of his life was open to scrutiny by the young Jesuits he was guiding. They didn't just listen to what he said; they also paid attention to what he did over the course of each day that he was together with them in community. It also meant that he had to judge difficult situations with a lot of wisdom. For instance, sometimes it might become apparent that a young man in studies did not have had the temperament or gifts to exercise ministry as a Jesuit. The resulting struggle could make life difficult for the individual himself, of course, but it could also become burdensome for his companions in community. In his role as formator, Michael Paul occasionally had to set young men free from this burden, all the while making it clear that he wasn't rejecting them. All this required time, energy and tremendous tact, but it frequently bore fruit in a new-found happiness in those who left to follow another path.

I was one of the young Jesuits whom Michael Paul formed. When I was nineteen years old, and had just finished my two-year Jesuit novitiate, I moved into the same community as Michael Paul, who was in his early forties at that time. We spent the next three years as companions under the same roof. Michael Paul was both a father-figure and a friend: a father-figure because of his age, experience and the wisdom he dispensed at just the right moment; a friend because he was close, always available and a true companion. Whenever I shared my youthful struggles with him, he always gave me his complete attention. He listened in such a way that it was easy for me to open up, and frequently to say much more than I had originally planned. In those moments he manifested, in word and gesture, his deep reverence for what he saw of God within me.

That's what stands out for me in a special way when I recall Michael Paul: his sense of reverence, both for God and for people. A reverent person looks at everyone with a deep sense of respect: with enough distance to allow people to be free to be themselves, and with enough closeness to be filled with wonder at the hidden mystery. Reverence is an excellent antidote to self-absorption, because a reverent person marvels so much at the wonder of what they encounter that they have little time to think of themselves. Helen Keller once said that 'the only thing worse than being blind is having sight but no vision'. Michael Paul was visionary, and his vision was large enough to discern goodness in all sorts of unexpected places. His sense of reverence was linked to his intuition that there was something too deep for words present in all that he experienced. This 'something' was the God he sought to find in all things, the God whose own Word gushes forth from a deep well of silence.

# CHAPTER TWO
# UNBELIEF

I have come to recognise that reverence is a key to faith. I may have to wait through dark moods before being able to re-enter that reverence. I may have to put up with myself as I stand sulking outside. But eventually I get in touch again and rediscover a wisdom that is in tune with my deepest human experience. I have stopped being surprised by my bouts of doubt. They come and go like the Irish weather; indeed, they are very much linked with inner weather. My prayer becomes that great phrase of King Lear: 'Sweeten my imagination'. Which means waiting for the return of light. Whenever I am in touch with love, with the giving self, with the goodness of people even in darkness, then faith makes sense. ***Where is Your God?***

Unbelief now has become for many an inherited confusion, a distance from roots, a cultural by-product, an undramatic limbo of indifference. Moreover, this religious vacuum is part of a larger unease and uncertainty about values, about institutions, about the very possibility of finding liveable meanings. ***What Are They Saying About Unbelief?***

In April 1974 Michael Paul published a controversial article in the periodical *The Furrow*, with the provocative title, 'Atheism Irish Style'. At a time when the general consensus held that Irish Catholicism was in a healthy state, Michael Paul alarmed many by suggesting that it was actually dying a slow death.

*A Provocative Article*

He claimed that Irish Catholics – and most of all young Irish Catholics – were becoming increasingly disillusioned with many of the externals of Church life: religion taught impersonally or in an authoritarian manner in school, dull Sunday rituals and boring sermons. At that time, huge emphasis was placed on attendance at Mass as a sign of a healthy Church, whereas, in Michael Paul's analysis, this practice was spiritually impoverished, having little prayerfulness, no sense of living worship and no real attempt to create a human community. The article, as well as subsequent talks and interviews he gave, generated widespread discussion and debate.

With this article, Michael Paul made his debut as a commentator on the phenomenon of unbelief. In many ways, it typified the approach he was to take throughout his writing career. He didn't seek to defend faith in the face of arguments against it, but rather to explain how faith could be disappearing before our eyes without our realising it. Additionally, he pointed out that the failures of Christians and of the Church were contributing causes to unbelief. In the article, he quoted the opening line of a short story by Brian Moore that recounts the writer's experience of being brought up as a Catholic in Belfast: 'In the beginning was the word and the word was No'.

Like Moore himself in this witty line, Michael Paul had a facility for exposing the moralistic and unhealthy aspects of religion in a way that didn't antagonise his readers. In his gentle way, he took on the role of a 'Socratic gadfly' with his fellow Christians. In a similar way to the ancient Greek philosopher Socrates, who pictured the city of Athens as a somewhat noble yet sluggish steed that needed to be stung into life, so Michael Paul took on the role of a benign horsefly who posed the kinds of questions designed to puncture the smugness and complacency of professed Christians.

## Doctorate in Belfast

Impressed by his innovative contribution to the public conversation on faith in Ireland, Michael Paul's superiors urged him in the mid-1970s to undertake a doctorate in theology. Having already published articles about the emergence of unbelief among Irish youth, he himself felt drawn now toward exploring the phenomenon of atheism in a more systematic way. After obtaining a year's leave of absence from the Department of English in UCD, he enrolled as a PhD student at Queen's University, Belfast, in 1978. As a result of his research he became the first Roman Catholic ever to be awarded a doctorate in theology by Queen's.

Entitled *Approaches to Unbelief*, Michael Paul's thesis reflects his particular style of thinking. Rather than studying one precise area in a specialised way, the thesis ranges across a wide horizon. The same approach is to be found in his books. He always preferred the freedom of a broad-ranging and comparative investigation to the prospect of being tied down by a narrow focus. It is worth drawing attention to some of the many interesting points he makes in his dissertation.

## Exploring the Second Vatican Council

Michael Paul's thesis presents a selective history of how believers have responded to unbelief, starting with the Second Vatican Council (1962-1965). As Bishop Schmitt of France remarked during that Council, 'For the first time in the history of the Church, a Council is meeting in an age of atheism'. Interestingly, when the Council Fathers first came together in October 1962, there was hardly any mention of atheism; yet three years later, just four days before the Council came to a close in December 1965, a huge majority approved the first ever conciliar statement to respond – in a sympathetic and pastoral manner – to atheism.

What stands out above all in the Council's approach to atheism is the new tone it adopted, a tone which shaped the way theologians and pastors responded to the lack of faith in the following years and decades. First, the Council showed that the Church was aware of how complex atheism is. Until then, atheism had mostly been considered in the context of Communism, but now the Church saw that atheism wasn't limited to the Communist sphere. Second, it showed that the Church wanted to approach atheism in a sympathetic way. Third, it demonstrated that the Church was open and willing to engage in dialogue with unbelievers. Taken together, these three developments amounted to the end of an antagonistic or superior attitude in the face of atheism. The Church exhibited real humility, admitting that the failure of Christians to live Christian lives often gave rise to atheism.

## A Key Insight

After exploring the findings of the Second Vatican Council, Michael Paul's dissertation goes on to examine how unbelief is analysed by the distinguished Jesuit theologian, Karl Rahner. This second chapter of Michael Paul's thesis is the most speculative and theoretical part of all. Nevertheless, he picks up an amazing insight from Rahner, an insight he himself was to use again and again, not only in his writing, but also in his work with young people. This insight is not about the content of what we believe, but is connected with how we present the faith today. While the truth abides and remains the same, the culture we live continually changes, so we need to express the same age-old truths in a language that is fresh and new. It makes little sense to cling stubbornly to a particular formula if it no longer conveys what we are trying to communicate. Paradoxically, in order to communicate something that has not changed, we need to change the way we speak about it.

To convey his fascinating insight, the German theologian Karl Rahner uses a bewildering term, 'mystagogy'. The word itself comes from a Greek word, which means to be led into the mysteries, and it expresses Rahner's key concern about how to initiate people into an experience of God today. His basic idea is simple: it is necessary to find and name some signs of God's presence in a person's experience before telling that person about the Good News. Or, to put it slightly differently, people must first identify the signs of God's presence in their lives before they can connect these divine signs with the message of the gospel.

Our culture is into experience, rather than doctrines, rules or principles. Like Karl Rahner, Michael Paul saw that people hadn't time for abstruse theology or endless speculation. They wanted a direct experience of God instead. The mystagogical approach suggests where to start when leading people into the mystery of Christianity, and the best place is where they are themselves – their own lives and their own experiences, perceived as graced experiences. Mystagogy is a way of awakening the spiritual dimension that is often dormant inside us. It does this by creatively connecting with our innate capacity to experience God. The beginning of one of the landmark documents of the Second Vatican Council, *Gaudium et Spes* – the Pastoral Constitution on the Church in the Modern World – endorses this mystagogical approach, by declaring that the joys and hopes, the sorrows and anxieties of the people of today must be accepted by the disciples of Christ as their concerns too. These griefs and joys are not to be scorned or dismissed; they are not irrelevant or unimportant. On the contrary, the experience of human beings today must be the starting point for Christian theology and for concrete Christian service.

Pope Francis, with his knack for straightforward language, gives a particularly clear description of the starting point of mystagogy, in his interview with Antonio Spadaro SJ in August 2013. 'I have a dogmatic certainty,' says the Pope, 'that God is in every person's life. God is in everyone's life. Even if the life of a person has been a disaster, even if it is destroyed by vices, drugs or anything else – God is in this person's life. You can, you must try to seek God in every human life. Although the life of a person is a land full of thorns and weeds, there is always a space in which the good seed can grow. You have to trust God.'

At the heart of mystagogy is the desire to open people to an experience of God, rather than just 'heady' knowledge of God. Michael Paul came to this experience of God in several ways: through the spirituality of Ignatius Loyola, through regular personal prayer and through his participation in the Charismatic Renewal. But he also came to glimpse God in the imaginative language of poetry and literature, most particularly in the poetry of George Herbert.

Because of his love for words and literature, Michael Paul realised that mystagogy demanded the crafting of words that truly speak. Too often, religious language is dead in the sense that it doesn't resonate or touch hearts. If our language becomes too routine, too mundane and too commonplace, it loses its power to affect and to transform. The Second Person of the Blessed Trinity is the Word, and because of the Word, words are sacred. It was through words that the world came into being in the first place. Words are not mere instruments to communicate, but are themselves creative. They can open a pathway to something deep inside, to God's presence.

Michael Paul realised that language is sacramental, that it can evoke something mysterious and transcendent, and somehow even contain that mysterious something in itself. Words, when used with care and imagination, can allow us to get in touch with the mysterious quality of reality. There is mystery in created reality because it contains signs and signature marks of the one who created it. Images and symbols touch our minds, hearts, emotions and wills: they speak to the whole person. Michael Paul discovered new symbols in literature, symbols that had a freshness that captured the deeper layers of human experience where God is present. We'll see shortly how Michael Paul used a mystagogical approach with students who were struggling to believe. But for now, let's return to his thesis.

## A New Paganism

In the second chapter of his thesis, Michael Paul gives a short account of the approach to unbelief as understood in the World Council of Churches. He draws attention to certain insights of W. A. Visser 't Hooft, long-time Secretary General of the World Council of Churches. In his summary, Michael Paul draws attention to Visser 't Hooft's description of Europe as neo-pagan. In his opinion, Europe was neither Christian nor atheist, but rather was embracing a new kind of paganism.

Visser 't Hooft's claim has largely been vindicated over the last number of decades. Many Europeans have abandoned the Bible, forgotten the liberating story of Christianity, and lost hope in the next life. At the same time, many are going back to something of the pagan origins that predate Christianity. In a sense, Europe is moving away from the place to which Christianity brought it, and moving back towards where it was when Christianity first arrived on our shores. Today, we do not find much philosophical atheism or militant atheism – apart from a minority of well-known figures such as Richard Dawkins – but instead a kind of practical atheism, a tendency to leave religion aside and not even think of God. It's not an all-out war against God, but a steady haemorrhaging of faith. Europe has become a continent where God is irrelevant in the lives of a great many people. Carl Jung once said that Christianity in Europe was similar to a cathedral that was built above a pagan temple. In other words, the roots of Christianity may not have gone down deeply at all.

Visser 't Hooft realised that some forms of neo-paganism in Europe caricature Christianity as a faith that denies life, represses our natural drives, and is the kind of spoilsport that tries to kill our sense of joy. This leads to paganism being viewed as healthy and life-giving, in contrast with Christianity, which is derided as neurotic and dysfunctional. Visser 't Hooft emphasised the importance of recovering a true image of Christianity as leading to the fullness of life: 'I have come that they may have life and life in abundance' (*Jn 10:10*).

## Research from Quebec

From a practical and pastoral point of view, Chapter Six is the most illuminating chapter of Michael Paul's thesis. Here he relates the findings of the Catholic Secretariat for non-believers in Montreal, Canada. Until the late fifties, French-speaking Quebec was a highly church-going society. Then, in fewer than twenty years, a seismic transformation took place with huge social changes. In the political arena, schools and hospitals moved from Church to State control, and the Quebec nationalist movement grew. In the economic sphere, consumerism, industrialisation and urbanisation increased. On the communication front, television became hugely influential. Meanwhile, the Catholic Church became increasingly marginal, and the young generation abandoned organised religion. By 1970 a whole new generation of Quebecois grew up without setting foot inside a church.

The Montreal Secretariat was especially interested in analysing why people abandoned religious practice. Its team was struck by the fact that many people, without actually denying God's existence, in practice lived as though God did not exist. Although some priests consoled themselves with the thought that Catholics who had stopped practising still kept the faith, researchers at the Secretariat asked a tough question: 'What faith, if any, were they actually keeping?' In certain ways, the massive fall-off in religious practice in Ireland has echoes of the Quebecois experience.

The Montreal researchers found that there was a typical progression toward unbelief. It began with people ceasing to practise their faith, because they no longer found it meant much to them. This led to their separation from the Church, to which they no longer felt they belonged, thinking of themselves as outsiders. Finally, they made their own selection from the teachings of the Church. The researchers concluded that the apparent previous strength of Catholic practice actually hid a lack of personal commitment. In other words, much of the previous practice may have been largely a matter of conformity, of attending Mass because that was what one was expected to do. The researchers also predicted that faith would probably not last in those individuals who had abandoned religious practice.

André Charron, the chief researcher at the Montreal Secretariat, divided the majority of unbelievers into two groups. The first group he called 'free-lance believers', the second 'unbelievers'. Free-lance believers have faith in some kind of God, but as a rule they cannot accept a personal God. Instead they acknowledge God as something like the cause of the universe or an impersonal force. They often feel disappointed with faith or with the Church, and steadily leave faith aside because religion seems irrelevant to them. They often find greater satisfaction in values outside of Catholicism, such as political involvement or belief in social progress.

The second group identified by Charron includes people who are so preoccupied with making ends meet or so taken up with the pressures of living that the religious dimension of life doesn't even surface for them. There is nothing agonised about their unbelief, and they at least seem at ease with it. This kind of unbelief may result from their fixation on material concerns, or it may be due to social reasons, for instance, the fact that many of their peers have stopped practising. Alternatively, it may result from their failure to find any psychological or personal anchor in faith.

Charron describes eight distinct steps in a person's move away from faith. It starts with moving away from attending Mass. Then the person steps away from the Church as an institution. Next, the Church as a community becomes distant. Following that, Christian practices and actions are dropped. Subsequently, the person stops seeing life in Christian terms. Next, the person moves away from a relationship with Jesus. When that happens, faith in a personal God grows dim. Finally, thought about religion ceases entirely.

The Montreal Secretariat also benefited from the psychological workshops developed by Léopold de Reyes. These workshops were intended to help pastoral workers and teachers to communicate with various kinds of unbelievers. Léopold de Reyes found insights in the school of psychology called 'transactional analysis' that were especially valuable for contact between believers and unbelievers. Transactional analysis categorises human interaction into three different states: the parent, the adult and the child. In his research, de Reyes found that many unbelievers experience believers as too rigid and authoritarian (the parent), too intellectual (the adult) and either aggressive or naïvely emotional (the child) in the way they present their faith. In order to improve the quality of dialogue, de Reyes brought these aspects to light. His most important discovery was that in any dialogue between believers and unbelievers, the most essential aspect is not the content of the dialogue itself, but the relationship between the two persons, a relationship characterised by mutual freedom and respect between equals. If there is not a good relationship between the believer and unbeliever, then the ideas and convictions of the believer will be largely irrelevant.

*Insights from Literature*
In the final chapter of his thesis, Michael Paul asks what kind of insights literature could usefully bring to the human experience of

religious questioning. He focuses on two novelists from different centuries and very different countries, the Russian Fyodor Dostoevsky (1821–81) and the Australian Patrick White (1912–90).

There is no doubt that Dostoevsky stands head and shoulders above all other novelists in terms of the depth with which he presents and responds to atheism. The change in tone initiated by the Second Vatican Council is already foreshadowed in Dostoevsky's writings: atheism is no longer viewed in an abstract and judgmental way, but as a human phenomenon that must be understood in its personal and cultural reality. This strongly existential emphasis is at the heart of Dostoevsky's exploration of atheism.

In 1868 Dostoevsky declared that he would write a long novel about atheism. He wanted to give a dramatic account of the huge impact of the loss of faith on a man in his mid-forties. He confessed that this planned novel had its roots in his own struggles with faith. In one of his letters, Dostoevsky commented, 'The fundamental idea, which will run through each of the parts, is one that has tormented me, consciously and unconsciously, all my life long: it is the question of the existence of God'. Indeed, in one of the last letters he ever wrote, in January 1881, Dostoevsky explicitly connects his portrayal of the Grand Inquisitor in the novel *The Brothers Karamazov* with his own inner tensions: 'Even in Europe such force of atheistic expression does not now exist nor did it ever. Accordingly, it is not like a child that I believe in Christ and profess faith in him, but rather, my hosanna has come through the greatest crucible of doubt.'

In *The Brothers Karamazov*, Dostoevsky gives full imaginative freedom to the atheistic view of things, so much so that some commentators claim that the case for atheism in the novel is in fact stronger than the case for faith. Simplifying things a lot, here are the two sides in the fictional debate in *The Brothers Karamazov*. On the one side is Ivan Karamazov. He takes a stand against God and against the world created by God for two reasons: the cruelty inflicted on the weak by their fellow human beings and the betrayal of Christ by organised religion. It is the passionate intensity with which Ivan expresses these arguments that makes them so powerful.

On the other side is the monk Zossima whose ideas, because they are developed with much less concreteness and intensity than those of Karamazov, are less effective from a dramatic point of view. Zossima gives voice to Dostoevsky's own favourite ideas on the origins of atheism, suggesting that it stems from isolation from others and from the inability to love. Tellingly, the epigraph in *The Brothers Karamazov* is taken from the Gospel of John, where it says that unless a grain of wheat falls into the ground and dies, it remains alone (*Jn 12:24*). All of Dostoevsky's atheists are alone, isolated and disconnected from others. In this way, Dostoevsky doesn't respond to atheism in a theoretical manner but in terms of relationships. He is convinced that the presence of a relationship is a stronger response than any purely intellectual argument.

The main lesson that Michael Paul draws from Dostoevsky's fictional treatment of atheism is the humbling sense of human complexity it offers, a complexity that transcends our desire for neat and tidy ways of understanding atheism. The literary expression of unbelief has a power that cannot be found in more theoretical analyses. It portrays the ambiguity of experience without trying to force too much clarity upon it. And when the literary imagination is set free in this way, it does not allow itself to be reduced to narrow or stereotyped judgments.

As well as showing the prophetic capacity of literature to be in advance of theoretical thought when it comes to atheism, Dostoevsky's fiction also demonstrates the greater persuasive power of image over concept in any dialogue between belief and unbelief. Furthermore, Dostoevsky gives us a privileged view of how atheism and faith are experienced in the heart, rather than as theory. Ultimately, Dostoevsky's treatment of atheism through fiction confirms a significant shift that marks the whole contemporary approach to atheism. It is the shift from doctrine to life, from the intellectual level to the level that precedes concepts, from metaphysical theories to a concrete understanding of what it means to be human. Dostoevsky's novels act as a reality check for approaches that are too theoretical. His novels do this by portraying flesh and blood human beings in all their ambiguity. It was exactly this kind of approach that Michael Paul would adopt in his writing and in his ministry.

Michael Paul was struck by the deep-seated religious concern that continued to characterise literature after Dostoevsky. Twentieth-century imaginative literature, even the literature written by unbelievers, was oftentimes a means of spiritual exploration. Although the religious question was not posed in the same overt way we find in Dostoevsky's novels, it did continue to dominate literature. The very possibility of having a religious horizon became a major concern. The focus wasn't on the arguments of atheism, but more on a frustrated religiousness. Often, the question was framed along the following lines: how can a religious attitude or spiritual way of being survive in a world that seems to have gone completely secular?

In one of his lectures, T. S. Eliot made a remark concerning certain novelists which can be seen to have a wider application. Eliot noted that they showed 'indifference to religious dogma and at the same time exceptional awareness of spiritual reality'. Nineteenth-century literature openly referred to the disappearance of God; twentieth-century literature took a step back – to the prior level of the disappearance of wonder and mystery, to the shrinking of the spiritual horizon. In addition, even when literature isn't overtly spiritual, it still has a unique power to open the dimension of wonder for readers, because it uses images to communicate, and these images often provide a covert spiritual experience.

Over the course of two decades – between 1955 and 1976 – Patrick White published a series of seven major novels which are unified by a common exploration of the question of religion and spirituality in an age of unbelief. His novels are preoccupied with the challenge, as well as the necessity, of reaching a sense of God. Referring to this religious sense in his writings, White said revealingly, 'Religion. Yes, that's behind all my books. What I am interested in is the relationship between the blundering human being and God. I belong to no Church, but I have a religious faith.' Patrick White believed that everyone had some kind of religious faith, or at least the seeds of it, but that many 'are either too lazy, or too frightened, or too ashamed intellectually to accept the fact'. White himself didn't pay much attention to his own religious tendencies until writing *The Tree of Man*, which was published in 1955, and is the first in this cycle of seven novels.

For Michael Paul, Patrick White's novels exemplify in a powerful way what Karl Rahner means by mystagogy: his novels awaken readers to a sense of mystery. The novel *Riders in the Chariot* (1961) exemplifies the cost of becoming aware that 'everything, finally, was a source of wonder, not to say love'. Whereas Dostoevsky in *The Brothers Karamazov* dramatises the conflict of decision about Jesus, Patrick White steps further back to the conditions of heart – wonder and mystery – that are necessary for faith. In the climactic scene of *The Solid Mandala* (1966), Arthur dances in front of Mrs Poulter to show her the religiousness he has found: 'Even in the absence of gods, his life, or dance, was always prayerful'. In *The Eye of the Storm* (1973), Elizabeth Hunter has a defining memory of escaping death through being in the eye of the storm, a moment when she experienced transcendence. While Dostoevsky defended faith against his own dramatic portrayal of atheism, White defends mystery and the quest for God against a cultural background dominated by mediocrity. In the novel *Voss* (1957), the rampant mediocrity of Australian middle-class society is attacked, and we find the following revealing comment: 'Only a few stubborn ones will blunder on, painfully, out of the luxuriant world of their pretensions into the desert of mortification and reward'.

## Help My Unbelief

In 1983 Michael Paul published his first, and most famous book, *Help My Unbelief*, aimed at readers who were bewildered at why God was becoming so unreal for them. The book sold extremely well because of Michael Paul's eleventh-hour appearance on Ireland's most popular television programme at the time, *The Late Late Show*. The celebrity who had been due to be interviewed became ill, and Michael Paul was called upon at the last minute to replace him. His appearance made a significant impact.

In this book, Michael Paul's focus was not on intellectual arguments for or against God, because he did not believe this was where the real story was. He concentrated instead on dispositions and basic attitudes. He was canny enough to know that people do not make decisions about faith based upon purely rational grounds. Our decisions for or against faith generally involve a strong sense of how we feel about ourselves and life. He was convinced that most blockages to faith were not on the level of intellect or doctrine, but of inner freedom. As a result, the search for religious truth is only possible if a person has an open disposition, and this openness cannot be unlocked through complex arguments.

He gave the example of a college student who came into his office to discuss an essay one day. Suddenly the student paused and announced in a belligerent voice, 'I'm an atheist, you know'. When Michael Paul ignored this declaration, and continued to give him feedback on his essay, the student asked, 'Aren't you supposed to try to convert me?' Michael Paul found himself responding, 'I wouldn't even think of converting anyone in that tone of voice', and went on to explain that faith was so important to him that he wouldn't dream of getting distracted by a useless argument about it. But if the student were ready to listen, he would be more than happy at some other time to explain what faith meant to him.

Sure enough, a few days later, the student returned. The atmosphere was tense to start off with, although Michael Paul realised that the student's return already spoke volumes. The young man then declared that there was something delicate he had to reveal about himself. He spoke about this and that for a while, and finally said, 'I suffer from asthma'. Michael Paul waited, presuming that there was something more sensitive to follow, but in fact it turned out that this was almost the entire story. The student went on to share how asthma had destroyed his childhood because it had cut him off from other people and had made him ashamed. He was angry at God and life. This story taught Michael Paul something crucial: behind many aggressive denials of faith ('I'm an atheist') there can be a much less aggressive reality of hurt and disenchantment ('I suffer from asthma').

In *Help My Unbelief*, Michael Paul pointed out something that many Church leaders had failed to see: that the major strength of Irish Catholicism – the immense faithfulness to Mass attendance – could quickly become its major weakness, if it never went beyond being simply an inherited way of behaving. He realised that high levels of practice were making bishops and priests complacent, leading them to forget the new needs that were emerging among those coming to Church and to ignore the hard questions of those who had ceased to practice. Mass attendance was becoming problematic for many, because it was in fact their only explicitly religious activity, and it was not being supported by other aspects of their daily lives.

The celebration of Sunday Mass, instead of being the high note of a week lived at a Christian pitch, can rapidly become hollow and boring if it is the sole occasion in the week for God to be acknowledged. The hollowness and boredom can be blamed on poor sermons, of course, or on liturgies that lack reverence and imagination. But boredom is also something that people bring with them as they cross the threshold of the church with small hearts (little experience of praying), small minds (a shallow understanding of their faith) and small hands (little to bring from the experience and activities of the week). Reflecting on the direction of Irish culture in general, Michael Paul saw that Ireland was moving from a culture of convention, where Catholics simply accepted what had been passed on from previous generations, to a culture of conviction, where they now had to find the truth for themselves. Rather than a language of obedience ('We must attend Mass every Sunday') people were turning to a language of experience ('I find it boring') and of relevance ('It doesn't mean anything to me'). Drawing on the research he had carried out for his doctoral thesis, Michael Paul identified the typical steps through which people move away from their faith, beginning with a decline in Mass attendance and a distancing from the Church community, and ending with a loss of faith in a personal God and the disappearance of religious questioning.

## The Struggle for Faith Today

Michael Paul began to study unbelief and atheism because of his passion to make faith meaningful for people, especially for those who had become distanced from the Church and from religion. Throughout his adult life he had friends who were unable to believe. He counted their friendship and their questions as true blessings. The example of their goodness frequently challenged Michael Paul to live his own faith in a more authentic way. He was honest enough to admit that he was not without doubts himself; he oscillated between a deep gratitude for the fullness of life and a begrudging attitude when he came up against the God's unexpected ways. This struggle between faith and doubt is in some sense everyone's story, and is forcefully expressed in a key document from the thirty-fourth General Congregation of the Jesuits in 1995: 'The boundary line between the Gospel and the modern and post-modern consciousness passes through the heart of each of us. Each Jesuit encounters the impulse to unbelief first in himself; it is only when we deal with this dimension in ourselves that we can speak to others of the reality of God.'

In his penultimate book, *Faith Maps*, Michael Paul speaks of faith in contemporary Ireland. In it he borrows an insight from Friedrich von Hügel, who was writing in the early twentieth century. He mentions three dimensions of faith as outlined by von Hügel: the institutional, the critical and the mystical, roughly corresponding to the three ages in life: childhood, youth and adulthood. Children are content to belong and to believe because of what their parents and teachers say. Faith is largely institutional at this stage. As they grow older, young people begin to ask questions, however, and want to work things out for themselves. Faith has to make sense of the way they experience life, and so they need a more critical faith. Then, in the adult stage, people move towards a more mystical phase where they need to experience the truth of religion in a deeply felt way. Not satisfied with merely belonging or figuring it out, people at this stage want to love and live what they believe.

In Michael Paul's analysis, many Irish people have left behind the institutional phase and have entered the second phase, where they are asking searching and critical questions about their faith. And some are also approaching the third stage, he believed, experiencing a real hunger for inner nourishment and for something that answers the heart's deepest longings. As Karl Rahner once put it, 'The believer of the future will be a mystic or will not exist at all'.

# CHAPTER THREE
## CULTURE

The greatest victory for the consumer ideology is to reduce religion to one more item on the supermarket shelf, making Christianity compete in the supply and demand of comforts and assurances. Thus a little bit of religion can become a most successful *musak* or background feeling for a life of fundamental drift or immaturity. This tranquillising use of religion for human security is the most typical trap of the first world. Christianity is turned into a pleasant evasion of reality, personally consoling but unchallenging socially, attractive for quick uplift and even a certain generosity, but avoiding the depths of discipleship as a choice within today's world. ***Free to Believe***

Perhaps the greatest danger to our humanity within today's culture lies in being disconnected from our depths. Within each person is a whole cluster of capacities of the heart – for wonder, searching, listening, receptivity, and life options for compassion and love. These are spiritual dimensions in everyone and they constitute the basis for the hearing from which faith is born. But one by-product of the fragmentations and pressures of today is that this whole zone can remain underdeveloped ... In the language of the Parable of the Sower, culture can become a multifaceted enemy for faith – robbing the seed, making shallow the roots, or choking the fragile plant. ***Clashing Symbols***

ichael Paul was a man of culture. He loved going to the theatre and the cinema, he knew the classic works of literature well, and he remained a constant

reader of contemporary authors also. Culture, in this sense of the term, covers great human achievements in literature, music, theatre and the visual arts. This is the understanding of culture espoused by the nineteenth-century English poet, Matthew Arnold, who maintained that culture meant pursuing perfection of the mind and the spirit through immersion in the greatest ideas in world history and literature. Michael Paul was especially appreciative of culture in this sense; yet he knew that what affected people most was 'culture' in a different sense: culture as 'the set of meanings and values that informs a way of life', as the Canadian Jesuit, Bernard Lonergan, put it.

## A New Awakening

From 1986 to 1987, Michael Paul spent a year's sabbatical in Latin America, and it was there that he came to see most clearly how it is our way of living, rather than our ideas, that decide whether we are open to religious faith or not. It was during this time that he came to appreciate the impact exerted by culture on people's lives. The highlight of his sabbatical was a month spent in Paraguay in 1987. There, he slept in a hut, heard countless confessions of the poor, and found that the Bible came alive in a new way through the voices of peasant women who led small Christian faith communities. Through these experiences, he felt an urge to expand his sense of Christianity beyond any narrow, individual focus.

In Asunción, Michael Paul got to know a seminarian called Eliseo. Along with his fellow seminarians, Eliseo organised a procession during Holy Week based on the Stations of the Cross. There is nothing unusual about religious processions in Latin America; they are a regular feature of Church life. This one was different, however, because the seminarians declared it would be in solidarity with the peasant leaders who had been thrown off their land and put into prison without trial.

It was obvious that this occasion was going to anger the authorities, and was likely to be yet another moment of conflict between the Catholic Church and the ruling regime over the plight of poor farmers. On Monday of Holy Week, the seminarians and staff began their procession at the seminary gates. Fifty metres from the gates, they were set upon by police in riot gear. The simple cross that had been made by peasants was broken, and the crown of thorns fell to the ground. In the melee that followed, thirty protesters were injured.

That evening, Eliseo told Michael Paul that, as the police hit him with their batons, his initial pain gave rise to anger. He felt an urge to hurl back insults at them. But then with his mind's eye he saw a scene from the film *Gandhi*, where the great leader of the Indian independence movement simply stood in a dignified way as blows came raining down upon him. Eliseo recalled saying to himself, 'If he could do this for the people of India, surely I can do it for Christ'. Once he had made this decision, Eliseo said, a deep sense of peace welled up inside him, despite the pain of the baton blows.

As the onslaught continued, Eliseo explained, the group retreated back behind the seminary gates. In the clashes, the helmet of a policeman had fallen and it landed next to Eliseo. What should he do? Keep it as a trophy of their struggle? As the group continued the Stations of the Cross within the gates of the seminary, Eliseo held on to the helmet, uncertain what to do with it. Then, as the prayers continued, he felt that same sense of peace inviting him to reach out, and so, after the procession, he stepped forward and handed the helmet back to the only policeman without one. The policeman grabbed it without any acknowledgement. Despite his disappointment, Eliseo had a sense that he and his friends were slowly – and painfully – making history, and that the truth of the gospel would eventually win out. From this incident, Michael Paul could see clearly that Eliseo's faith was not a private matter between God and himself; it was something that was alive in a shared way.

## The Communal Dimension

Stories like that of Eliseo helped Michael Paul to appreciate in a new way the importance of culture in the life of faith. He saw more clearly than ever that faith, far from being a private affair, can lead to conflict with the prevailing culture and with those forces that would have us believe that authority is never wrong. In fact, Michael Paul was deeply moved by the communal dimension of faith that he found throughout Latin America, making him regret more than ever the narrow individualism of so much in contemporary European culture.

One experience in particular summed up for him in an eloquent way the generous faith of the people. At one point, he was staying in a Jesuit community located in a large slum in San Félix, a city in the eastern part of Venezuela. Across the street from the Jesuit house was a poor family with about twelve children, one of whom would sometimes cross the road in the morning to see if any mangos had fallen from the tree during the course of the night. Pedro Pablo was fascinated by Michael Paul, this white man who spoke only broken Spanish, so they arranged to have regular Spanish-English conversation classes together.

One day, Michael Paul noticed that Pedro Pablo kept rubbing his stomach. When he asked him when he had last eaten, the boy said the previous morning. He asked if they had any food at home. 'Only a few mangos', the boy replied. With that, Michael Paul went into the kitchen, made a large sandwich, sat down next to Pedro Pablo and handed it to him. To his astonishment, the boy didn't eat a morsel. When asked why, the boy explained, 'I'm going to bring it to my mother who is pregnant'. And he set off, leaving Michael Paul shaken. For a long time he sat there, pondering and praying. He knew he had seen the Spirit of Jesus alive and thriving in this poor boy. It was one of those precious moments that carried him to the core of what life is all about.

Reading the Bible in Latin America also helped Michael Paul to see things afresh, with the Word of God catching fire for him in immensely challenging ways. For instance, although he had read the Letter of James many times in his life, but it wasn't until he read it in a prayerful way in San Félix that the frankness and forcefulness of this text truly came alive for him. In the second chapter, James comments that even the demons believe in God (*Jas 2:19*). James is making the point that belief in God can be completely disconnected from the way we live. We may believe, but if there is no love in our lives, our faith is simply dead. The whole of this chapter is an indictment of smug believers. James warns us not to show favouritism toward the rich (*2:1-4*). He points out that nice-sounding words are of no use to our needy brother or sister if they are not backed up by concrete actions to improve their situation (*2:1-17*). St James is profoundly distrustful of a faith that cannot be verified by deeds.

Many years later, Michael Paul had another experience that in some ways echoed his sabbatical year in Latin America. In the summer of 2014, he was invited to teach Jesuit students of theology in Vietnam. During his weeks in Saigon, he experienced a deep sense of happiness, occasioned by the profound experience of community he found there, once again a refreshing contrast to the barren individualism of the West. The Vietnamese people awoke a sense of joy and wonder in him that he felt he had almost lost. He was reminded of the words of the psalmist, 'My youth is renewed like the eagle's' (*Ps.103:5*). He used to say that if he were ten years younger, he would have asked to stay in Vietnam for good.

## A Critique of Culture

In his thinking on culture, Michael Paul was helped by the model of organisational culture developed by Edgar Schein. Schein is emeritus professor at MIT in Cambridge, Massachusetts, and an expert in the field of organisational development. He shows that if we really want to understand the way a culture works, we have to examine the deeply held assumptions that members of that culture share. Schein outlines three layers in organisational culture. The first layer, the layer of behaviour and artefacts, is the most obvious. It comprises things like the way people dress, their behaviour, the jokes they make, as well as the architecture and furniture of the places in which they live and work. The second layer, the layer of 'espoused values', includes the stated values and codes of behaviour of a group of people, as articulated in 'mission statements' and the like. The third layer, the level of deeply held tacit assumptions, is the most difficult layer to identify. These assumptions are so embedded and ingrained in people's lives that they often aren't even aware of them, particularly where it concerns their own culture; and yet they form the essence of their view of the world and their way of doing things.

Michael Paul extolled the apostle Paul as a master in the discernment of culture. Paul's speech at the Areopagus in Athens (*Acts 17:22-29*) is often cited as one of the finest examples in the New Testament of a Christian reaching out to pagan culture, showing the harmony between human hopes and God's message in Jesus Christ. The speech is indeed a stirring example of cultural outreach; but not too many people notice that the positive and generous tone of Paul's speech is totally at odds with his initial impressions of the city of Athens.

Indeed, Paul initially had a decidedly negative impression of Athens (*Acts 17:16-18*). We are told that Paul's 'whole soul was revolted at the sight of a city given over to idolatry'. He found that people there had a fondness for new, fashionable ideas that would amuse and distract them, and had little time for the message of Paul, whom they saw as 'a propagandist for some outlandish gods', and whom they mocked as a kind of 'parrot'. This was clearly a hostile environment and, with its cynicism and preoccupation with amusing novelties, a difficult culture to reach.

Given all of this, it is astonishing that Paul's speech (*Acts 17:22-28*) begins with him praising the people of Athens for being so religious. He mentions the altar to the Unknown God in the city, not as an example of idolatry, but as a sign that the Athenians have deep religious desires and hungers, and that they are actually worshipping the true God without knowing who the true God is. Paul then quotes from an ancient pagan poet – probably a native of his own town of Tarsus – when he observes that in God 'we live and move and have our being'. This poem was originally written in honour of the Greek god Zeus, yet Paul has no qualms about adopting it and re-applying it to the Christian God. Paul is trying to enter into the culture of the Athenian people. He is inviting them to embrace the Christian faith in a way that allows them to remain faithful to the authentic values of their own culture.

Paul then goes on to talk about our sense of reverence before creation, and the need to repent if we want to emerge from ignorance. When he starts speaking about the Resurrection from the dead, many people feel he has gone too far, however, and they start to laugh at him. Nevertheless, several people are willing to give him a second chance, and a few of them actually become Christians as a result of his speech.

Michael Paul believed that we can all learn from Paul. Often our first contact with a new culture can lead to negative reactions and to harsh judgments. We don't like what is different in what we find. The first things we encounter in another culture are usually the external things, and when we look at the externals, we easily judge the people of another culture as superficial or lost. We find ourselves doubting that God could be in any way present in these people or in their culture.

So, what happened with Paul? How did he move from his initial dislike to a much more open-minded approach? The *Acts of the*

*Apostles* doesn't give us any explanation of the change, so we can only speculate. Most likely he reflected and prayed, eventually arriving at a more positive way of seeing Athenian culture. He saw beneath the appearances, and ceased to be irritated by what he found on the surface. He looked for the deeper values. He no longer allowed himself to become upset at all the idols and statues that he saw as he walked around the city; instead he focused his attention on the spiritual hunger that these statues were expressing.

## A Trusting Disposition

Michael Paul was convinced that in order to evaluate any culture, we need a basic stance of openness. Beneath all forms of idolatry, he believed, there was some vestige of authentic spirituality. We need to be open to the deeper attitudes and desires of people, trusting in the goodness of reality and resisting the temptation to reject what we don't understand. This is not the same as being naïve. Certainly, there will be bad features present in all cultures, but no culture is beyond redemption. If we ourselves are filled with negativity, however, we won't be able to see the good in that particular culture. On the other hand, if we respond from a positive place of peace and equilibrium, even our criticisms will be allied to a sense of confidence that the flaws are only part of the picture. So, our own disposition and attitudes are vital.

Fundamentally, Michael Paul was convinced that God's grace could get through to everyone. That's why he wasn't afraid to go to 'the crossroads of ideologies', in the words of Pope Paul VI, to wherever a 'confrontation between the burning exigencies of the human being and the perennial message of the Gospel' was to be found. He didn't become bogged down by the polarisation of 'either-or', but instead sought to do justice to the catholicity of 'both-and'.

Fear-filled rhetoric and polarising arguments were never part of

Michael Paul's cultural analyses. In his view, by reacting to what is negative with our own negativity, we make ourselves unable to penetrate to its beauty and goodness. Our basic disposition must be one of trust, he believed, even when acknowledging the flaws and weaknesses we perceive. Nothing and nobody is beyond salvation, because the universe can never be neatly divided between good and evil, good guys and bad guys. Learning from the example of St Paul in the *Acts of the Apostles*, he insisted on viewing all cultures from a fundamental stance of hope. This helped him to find faith at the fringes, wavelengths of wonder in a spiritual wasteland, and openings for love amidst walls of egoism.

## The Two Standards

The roots of this approach can be found in the spirituality of St Ignatius, which formed Michael Paul from his novitiate years. It is a spirituality that is both highly hopeful and exceptionally realistic. It is hopeful, because Ignatius is convinced that God can be found in all things. It is realistic, because Ignatius also sees life as a constant struggle between the powers of good and evil. Ignatius urges his followers to becoming aware of the inner struggle that is taking place all the time between authentic and counterfeit values, between truthfulness and falsehood. The major battle that goes on in our hearts takes place, not at the level of arguments and ideas, but at the affective level.

In this decisive battle, Michael Paul was convinced that we must avoid becoming belligerent ourselves. Ironically, we can only 'fight' this inner battle with the weapons of peace. The invitation, then, is for us to live out of the deeper level of ourselves, where we feel in tune with who we really are, for it is there that we find the grace to deal serenely, not just with the struggles of our own hearts, but with the struggles of our culture as well. On the other hand, if we drift through life on a superficial level, reacting instinctively rather than responding gracefully, then we will be trapped by our immature selves, and aggression will never be far away.

One of the key meditations in the *Spiritual Exercises*, 'A Meditation on the Two Standards', is designed to help us distinguish better between the destructive patterns that can seduce the heart and the call of Jesus to a radically different way. When Ignatius speaks of two standards, he is using imagery that would have been readily understood in the sixteenth century. He is referring to the two flags or military banners which were carried by opposing armies in battle. In the confusion of war, each soldier, by looking toward the raised flag or standard, instantly knew where his leader was in order to rally around him. The meditation called by this name is intended to enlighten our minds, so that in the midst of the complexities of our busy lives, we can recognise the person of Jesus and rally to his call. Michael Paul prayed on this exercise many times during the course of his life.

In the Meditation on the Two Standards, Ignatius presents us with formidable imagery. On the one hand, he asks us to imagine the gently appealing figure of Christ standing in the vicinity of Jerusalem. On the other hand, we are presented with the terrifying figure of Lucifer, seated on a throne of fire near Babylon. The sharp contrast between the two figures signifies how opposed they truly are. Their strategies for our world are also totally opposed. Jesus is shown gathering his followers around him and inviting them to go out and attract people to embrace his vision. In contrast, Satan aggressively 'summons innumerable demons' to him, 'goading them' into laying snares for people. Then, having trapped them, they are to 'bind them with chains'. As St Ignatius presents this meditation, he makes it clear that no place, no person and no way of life is exempt from the competing claims of light and darkness. The battle is everywhere.

This meditation is deeply rooted in Scripture, of course. 'No one can serve two masters', says Jesus (*Mt 12:30*), and in the parable of the wheat and the weeds Jesus makes it clear that both good and evil are entangled together in this life (*Mt 13:24-30*). By opposing Jerusalem and Babylon, Ignatius is echoing the imagery of the *Book of Revelation*, which challenges us to choose either the peace, humility and goodness of the New Jerusalem or the violent and arrogant opulence of Babylon. This vision of two opposing cities was later immortalised by St Augustine in his great work, *The City of God*: 'Two cities have been formed by two loves: the earthly by the love of self, even to the contempt of God; the heavenly by the love of God, even to the contempt of self.'

Despite the grandiose military imagery that Ignatius uses, the Meditation on the Two Standards is in fact about a battle that takes place primarily within our hearts. At this point in the Spiritual Exercises, the person making the retreat has already made a basic decision for Jesus. With this meditation, however, Ignatius wants to emphasise that the struggle is by no means over; it continues incessantly inside ourselves, at the level of our conflicting desires. We have to recommit ourselves to him again and again, because the battle is ongoing and we are always being drawn in contrary directions. We must repeatedly choose our standard and our leader.

In Ignatius's paradigm, the 'enemy of our human nature' tempts us powerfully, and often subtly, by playing on our greed for possessions and for the prestige and adulation that often accompany them. Satan's ultimate goal is to bring us to 'overweening pride', where God is effectively displaced by the self-absorbed individual. If this sounds like a summary of the message our consumerist society frequently transmits to us, it is surely a confirmation of the enduring relevance of Ignatius's insight.

The standard of Jesus is radically different. Jesus invites us to see that everything is gift. It doesn't make sense to measure ourselves in terms of possessions or power, because nothing is truly ours. All we have points to the Giver, who is our loving Father and will continue to provide us with what we need. Instead of saying 'Look at me', we are moved to say 'Look at God and all that God has done for me'. It is the message of the Beatitudes (*Mt 5:1-12*).

## Poverty of Spirit

Michael Paul sometimes recommended his friends to read a profound and beautiful little book on what it means to be human and vulnerable. The book is called *Poverty of Spirit* and it's by the German theologian Johannes Baptist Metz. In a similar vein to Ignatius, Metz maintains that we can either accept our poverty of spirit or else run away from it unto unhealthy forms of living. 'A person with grace', writes Metz, 'is someone who has been emptied, who stands impoverished before God, who has nothing to boast of … It is the doorway through which we must pass to become authentic human beings. Only through poverty of spirit do we draw near to God; only through it does God draw near to us.'

Michael Paul realised that our Western culture can push us to resist humility in powerful ways. Yet, until we face our own poverty, we won't be truly ready for faith. Until we learn to have reverence for a mystery that far surpasses us, we will never be free to open ourselves to God's surprising ways. By wanting to find life without losing it first (*Mt 16:25*), we lose out on the truth that can really set us free. One of the most illuminating moments on the journey of faith is the realisation that, paradoxically, strength is to be found in weakness (*2 Cor 6:10*). The seventeenth-century mystic, philosopher and mathematician Blaise Pascal expressed it well: 'Knowledge of God without knowing our own poverty makes for pride. Knowledge of our own poverty without knowing God makes for despair. Knowledge of Jesus Christ lets us be present both to God and to our poverty.'

## Culture and Faith

Michael Paul liked to emphasise that each of us receives our faith in a particular cultural context. We are creatures of our culture, and that culture affects and influences the way we receive God's message. Faith is a response, our human 'yes' to God's prior divine 'yes'. Our small 'yes' echoes God's massive 'yes', but there are crucial differences. God's 'yes', fully embodied in Jesus, is eternal and lasting. Our 'yes' is much more precarious, much less steady, and often lacking focus. The culture we inhabit inevitably affects the quality of our 'yes' and has a huge impact on our faith. An old maxim from the philosophy of St Thomas Aquinas is truly pertinent here: *Quidquid recipitur ad modum recipientis recipitur* ('Whatever is received is received according to the manner of the receiver').

What we receive is affected by who we are and by where we find ourselves. Although Michael Paul didn't personally experience Irish Catholicism as repressive, he was aware that for many people of his generation it was associated with a petty vision, confined largely to external rules and narrow moralism. Irish Catholic leaders appeared to have forgotten that faith is about the fullness of life. As Frank McCourt wrote in *Angela's Ashes*, 'What are we to give up when we have Lent all year long?' This narrowness was already under scrutiny in a famous novel published over a hundred years ago. In the scene of the Christmas dinner from James Joyce's *A Portrait of the Artist as a Young Man*, Mr Dedalus exclaims, 'We are an unfortunate priest-ridden race and always were and always will be till the end of the chapter'. Today, just over a century later, it seems that we are indeed arriving at the end of the chapter, as Michael Paul, despite appearances to the contrary, anticipated presciently over forty years ago.

For most of the twentieth century, faith and culture practically coincided in Ireland. For the majority of the population, Catholicism was *the* way to live one's faith, and the notion of not believing seemed practically unreal. The imagery and symbolism of Catholicism touched people's lives, and provided them with an affective bond to their faith. In the next chapter, with the help of a poem by Seamus Heaney, we'll see how that whole cultural landscape changed.

# CHAPTER FOUR

# POETIC AND LITERARY PERSPECTIVES

The theologian Karl Rahner once claimed that 'the poetic is a basic need for Christianity': poetry awakens the depths; poetry speaks to the heart of our humanity; poetry forces us to stand honestly at the threshold of mystery. The hard-wrought words of [Gerard Manley] Hopkins have helped thousands and thousands towards that threshold, especially so in an age like ours that finds the usual languages of God unconvincing and distant. **Struggles of Faith**

If you pause and enter into yourself, if you can create a space of quiet self-presence, you get in touch with your longing for something more, even for something infinite. You discover yourself as a kind of mystery, limited in one little life, yet open to infinite horizons of questions and questings. **Faith Maps**

*I*t has already become evident that the vision embodied in literature and poetry constituted a vital element in Michael Paul's imaginative reservoir. Literature seldom deals with the Churches' response to unbelief, nor does it usually articulate what faith means for our day. Instead literature tends to concentrate on the interior spiritual drama. Unlike theologians, who always seek to give content to the mystery, poets and novelists are willing to remain on the level of mystery without needing to articulate it in words.

In Chapter Two we looked at how Michael Paul explored the fiction of Fyodor Dostoevsky and Patrick White in his doctoral dissertation. Patrick White experienced mystery even in the very composition of his novels. He describes how he felt that it was not he himself who wrote much of his best prose, but that he somehow felt it was 'being written' for him. In an address Patrick White gave to a conference in 1983 – several years after Michael Paul's doctoral thesis was written – he remarked, 'In the fourteenth century an anonymous English mystic wrote a book called *The Cloud of Unknowing*, the main theme of which is that God cannot be apprehended by man's intellect and that only love can pierce the "cloud of unknowing" which lies between him and us. I feel that in my own life anything I have done of possible worth has happened in spite of my gross, worldly self. I have been no more than the vessel used to convey ideas above my intellectual capacities. When people praise passages I have written, more often than not I can genuinely say, "Did I write that?" I don't think this is due to my having a bad memory, because I have almost total recall of trivialities. I see it as evidence of the part the supernatural plays in lives which would otherwise remain earthbound.'

## Literature and Theology

Michael Paul was convinced that literature embodied a world of wisdom that could truly enrich theology. Poets and novelists, like theologians, seek to touch mystery, something that eludes words but is not immune to the imagination. Ironically, some of the great classics of world literature actually express the mystery of what it means to be human in a more satisfying way than any theologian could possibly do. Michael Paul valued the way literature keeps the religious question alive in the human imagination. He was convinced that this was especially important because our Western culture can so easily stifle the riches of religious consciousness. He hoped that theologians would learn from novelists how to rediscover the richness of images and symbols, which are so effectively used by Jesus in his parables.

Although the literature of today displays little interest in organised religion, it does rescue our spiritual hungers by giving them dramatic expression. In a sense, literature, cinema and drama have become the unauthorized theology for our age of unbelief since, at their best, they succeed in capturing the depths of human experience with surprising power. They shine the light of religious wonder on our darkened times. Their success stems from the fact that the theoretical explanations of theology and the institutional structures of the Church easily leave our deepest hungers unmet and unnourished. The deepest truths resonate more readily for us when embodied in stories rather than dogmatic statements. As a result, the whole world of symbols, images and stories can take on a new significance for many people today.

In spite of all that, however, Michael Paul did not unquestioningly see literature as a realm of pure wisdom and light. In 1981, he published an article called 'The Gnostic Lure of Literature' in *The Month*. In it he wondered if modern literature, instead of being an entry into faith, might simply offer the glamour of spiritual discovery without any of the duties of religious commitment. He realised that literature was more comfortable with a vague sense of religiousness than with concrete commitment to any particular faith. He saw that literature loved staying with questions, and was reluctant to surrender itself to specific answers.

In addressing these issues, Michael Paul was clear that it is not the purpose of literature to draw readers into religious commitment. He believed that if there is a problem here, it lies, not with the creative artists themselves, but with those readers who are so enamoured by a world of images and symbols that they find themselves unable to commit themselves to any other kind of truth. Fictional truth appeals to the heart, which finds the language of imagination particularly satisfying. But that kind of language need not be an end in itself. It can lead beyond itself to commitment. Commitment, however, is demanding. To the extent that our culture promotes literature, cinema and art as the only forms of credible wisdom, the world of faith is set aside or excluded as a source of wisdom for the soul.

As for religion itself, it needs to find a way of presenting the truth that is not only credible for the mind, but appealing for the heart as well. Michael Paul would have been thoroughly familiar with the words attributed to the former Superior General of the Jesuits, Fr Pedro Arrupe (1907–91):

> Nothing is more practical than finding God, than falling in Love in a quite absolute, final way. What you are in love with, what seizes your imagination, will affect everything. It will decide what will get you out of bed in the morning, what you do with your evenings, how you spend your weekends, what you read, whom you know, what breaks your heart, and what amazes you with joy and gratitude. Fall in Love, stay in love, and it will decide everything.

Michael Paul wanted to help people to fall in love. Although working in the academic world, his instinctive focus was on the heart and the affections more than on the reason and the mind. Like Fr Arrupe, Michael Paul knew that it is love that gets us out of bed in the morning, and it is for that reason that he constantly drew attention to the affective dimension of life in his writings.

### Kindred Spirits
Poets are in love with words and language, which is why Oscar Wilde

could claim with some justice that 'a poet can survive everything except a misprint'. Arguably the greatest Irish poet of our time, Seamus Heaney was born in 1939, the same year as Michael Paul. Both came from the northwest of Ireland, though different counties. Seamus Heaney was born on a farm near Castledawson, a village in Co. Derry. Michael Paul, as we have seen, came from Collooney in Co. Sligo. Michael Paul counted this Nobel prizewinning poet as a friend and as a kindred spirit. They grew up in a similar kind of Ireland, and both noticed how rapidly and radically it had changed. Seamus Heaney died in August 2013, just two years before Michael Paul's own death.

Michael Paul warmed particularly to a poem of Seamus Heaney's with the curious Latin title, 'In Illo Tempore'. The poem evokes in a condensed and thought-provoking way the huge shift in Ireland's relationship to the Catholic faith over the last half-century or so. In this poem, Heaney portrays two different worlds: the wonder-filled world of childhood where faith fits, and a bleaker adult world where not only faith, but even life itself, has lost its point. It is not entirely clear if the narrator of the poem is Seamus Heaney himself, or if the poet is entering into someone else's experience. It is likely, however, that the speaker is close to, if not identical with, Heaney, for reasons that will soon become evident.

Michael Paul discussed this poem fleetingly in his book *Clashing Symbols*. Here I'm going to expand significantly on his brief comments, while hoping to remain as faithful as possible to how I believe Michael Paul himself would have reflected upon this poem.

> The big missal splayed
> and dangled silky ribbons
> of emerald and purple and watery white.
> Intransitively we would assist,
> confess, receive. The verbs

assumed us. We adored.

And we lifted our eyes to the nouns.

Altar-stone was dawn and monstrance noon,

the word 'rubric' itself a bloodshot sunset.

Now I live by a famous strand

where seabirds cry in the small hours

like incredible souls

and even the range wall of the promenade

that I press down on for conviction

hardly tempts me to credit it.

– from Station Island (1984)

The title of this poem is taken from the first words of the gospel as it was proclaimed in the old Latin Mass before the reforms of the Second Vatican Council. It seems that, whatever the reading of the day, the proclamation of the gospel at that time always began with the words *in illo tempore* – meaning 'at that time' – irrespective of whether those words were part of the reading or not. As the title suggests, the poem has a 'then and now' feel about it. The first section, comprising the first three stanzas, brings us back to the world of childhood wonder where faith makes sense. The remaining section reflects the adult world where the narrator has lost his spiritual moorings.

In the first stanza, Heaney paints a picture of a large, open missal on the altar, with its silky ribbons – 'emerald and purple and watery white' – hanging loosely from between its pages as markers.

The second stanza depicts faith as something that sustains and carries the whole community, something that doesn't need to be thought through or figured out: 'Intransitively we would assist, confess, receive'. There is a hint here – 'The verbs assumed us' – that this faith is inherited rather than personally acquired; nevertheless, it is a faith that is portrayed as authentic and real, because, to quote the second stanza again, 'we adored'. There is no compulsion evident in this adoration; instead there are the free personal acts of people who simply adored.

The third stanza highlights three key words: altar-stone, monstrance and rubric. Each of these is linked to successive moments over the span of the day: dawn, noon and sunset. Altar-stone is associated with the dawn, since Mass was celebrated only in the morning in those days. The monstrance, containing a large consecrated host, is often gold-plated and has rays emanating from its centre, making it like the noonday-sun in appearance. 'Rubric' originally referred to the red letters that focused attention on important sentences in medieval manuscripts. It later came to mean the regulations for conducting a religious service, usually printed in red in liturgical books. By associating 'rubric' with the 'bloodshot sunset', Heaney is probably linking it with the blood of Christ and with the host, which is round like the sun. The poet is suggesting that – in those days – the realm of the sacred enveloped the whole day.

Seamus Heaney is clearly drawing on his own memories in this poem. In an interview with Dennis O'Driscoll, published in *Stepping Stones: Interviews with Seamus Heaney*, he recalled how, at the age of twelve, he won a scholarship to St Columb's College in Derry, where the day began with Mass in Latin, and regular confession was the norm. Like most of his contemporaries, he would have been familiar with the items associated with the liturgy mentioned in the poem: altar-stone, missal, monstrance and rubric.

When we turn to the second part of the poem, we suddenly find ourselves in the world of the present. The fourth stanza, in fact, begins with the word 'now'. We have moved from the past to the present tense. The next word is also significant, because for the first time

Heaney uses the word 'I', a pronoun that does not appear in the first three stanzas. In those stanzas, it was a question of 'we' and 'us'. Now, it seems, all community support has vanished. There is no longer any group confessing, receiving or adoring. We find no mention of missals, monstrances, altar-stones or other sacred things with shared meaning. Instead, we find an individual who is alone and isolated. There is also a shift at this point from day to night, from light to darkness, as the speaker hears the sound of birds 'in the small hours'.

From a material point of view, the speaker is probably more secure now, since he lives 'by a famous strand'. Seamus Heaney lived near Sandymount Strand in an affluent Dublin suburb. The strand itself is, of course, famous in the literary world because of the prominence James Joyce gave it in *Ulysses*. But even here there is something disturbing about the sound of the seabirds, whose cries are reminiscent of unbelieving souls.

In the fifth and final stanza, the speaker is at a promenade. He presses down on the wall between the promenade and the sea, which should provide a shelter from the elements. Yet this solid reality doesn't offer him the support and security he needs. Even this tangible wall lacks credibility, and does not offer him the 'conviction' he so urgently seeks. He is unable to 'credit it'.

The poem ends on a note of sadness and despondency. The narrator is literally near the sea, but also figuratively at sea. There is no longer an anchor or a foundation. The speaker's life is lonely and adrift, a world away from his childhood innocence and faith. There is a sense of sadness at what has been lost, allied to a sense of bewilderment at what has taken its place.

### Then and Now

Both in Michael Paul's musings about culture, and in Seamus Heaney's poem, there is a sense of awakening to the realisation that there has been a huge shift in the way we live – a shift from a culture where it was practically impossible not to believe, at least in some rudimentary way, to a culture where belief is something we must struggle to acquire and to maintain. Sharing about his move away from his childhood faith in the interview with Dennis O'Driscoll, Seamus Heaney remarked that 'intellectually speaking, the loss of faith occurred offstage, there was never a scene where I had it out with myself or with another'. He goes on to say that the potency of words like 'transubstantiation' and 'real presence' remained for him: 'They retain an undying tremor and draw; I cannot disavow them. Nor can I make the act of faith.'

The loss which Heaney regrets is not something he planned or even anticipated. And neither is it that way for most of our contemporaries. Instead, it's something that they (and often we) inhale from the cultural air that surrounds us, something absorbed almost unconsciously. This loss happens without fanfare or drama, in an unspectacular and practically unnoticed way. As with Seamus Heaney, the loss of faith occurs offstage. And yet the loss is frequently not total. Heaney's openness to some kind of religiousness, with his simultaneous hesitation in the face of the demands of a particular religious faith, is reflected in many of our contemporaries. Karl Rahner expressed this well: 'All of us, even the atheist who is troubled and terrified by the agonising nothingness of his existence, seem to be able to be religious in the sense that we reverence the ineffable in silence, knowing that there is such a thing.'

It's revealing too that Seamus Heaney is still drawn by the power of words like 'transubstantiation' and 'real presence'. The wonder of his childhood faith has not vanished completely. At the very least, there is a certain indefinable something that still moves him deeply. He clearly recognises that there is more to reality than the visible, tangible world of the here-and-now that immediately surrounds us.

This is where Michael Paul enters the picture. When he found that people around him had lost the wonder of faith, he saw that they did not need more prose, in the sense of cold arguments in favour of faith, but a big dose of poetry instead, involving freshness, imagination and affectivity. As we have seen, the impetus for this approach began during the year he spent in Caen as a young man, where he discovered his gift for explaining the faith, not in the jargon of abstract argument, but by employing the living poetry of personal discovery.

Although most of us don't compose such amazing poems as Seamus Heaney did or analyse culture as incisively as Michael Paul, we still have some sense of the massive shift that has taken place in our way of living. It is obvious that we have new patterns of working, living, recreating and travelling. We're living in a culture where religious feasts no longer punctuate the rhythm of the year. In Ireland, we have moved from a culture in which it was frowned upon not to believe into a culture where belief is no longer taken for granted; from a culture where faith was a given to a culture where faith is difficult to arrive at and even more difficult to sustain.

'In Illo Tempore' gives a snapshot image of this inner dispositional shift. The speaker in the poem only notices this huge shift in his life after it has occurred, or perhaps it's only the consequences of that shift that he notices. And what is true of him at an individual level is also true of our culture. Michael Paul was fond of quoting what T. S. Eliot once said about faith during a radio talk he gave way back in 1945: 'The trouble of the modern age is not merely the inability to believe certain things about God which our forefathers believed, but the inability to feel towards God and man as they did'.

## The Searching Heart

Big thoughts need time to grow and mature, but unfortunately most of us today don't have a lot of time to cultivate depth. For instance, these days the internet is having a huge impact on us, but we are seldom conscious of how it dominates our lives. Whether we're at the bus stop or queuing up for a cup of coffee, we turn to our phones and mobile devices. We no longer bother memorising the telephone numbers of our friends because they are automatically stored in our own phones. Encyclopaedias have gone out of print, and we Google our information instead or turn to Wikipedia. No wonder Douglas Coupland, the Canadian novelist whose novels Michael Paul enjoyed, said, 'I miss my pre-internet brain'. Coupland believes that the internet is not only colonising our planet, but also our minds. We're all being affected by this colossal change, and probably because it's happening so fast, we haven't yet discovered a way to describe properly how it is affecting us.

What Michael Paul saw, sooner than most, was that the decisive change in Ireland was the change in context, the new cultural environment in which faith finds itself. Yet, despite this gigantic cultural shift, he was still convinced that God haunts every human heart and is at work in the adventure of every human life. He was inclined to believe that the pace of our lives and the focus of our attention were what kept us drifting on the surface of who we really are, and incapable of diving down to the deepest levels of ourselves. That's why he was impressed by authentic searchers; despite the pressures of the culture around them, they still searched for something deeper in their lives.

In this context, he was greatly encouraged by a creative new practice that he saw emerging in the Church, a practice he felt could purify theology in its perennial search for truth. On 27 October 2011, four prominent non-believers – among them the French writer and psychoanalyst Julia Kristeva – joined a large interreligious pilgrimage to Assisi at the express invitation of Pope Benedict XVI. Just a month previously, Benedict had praised genuinely searching agnostics, maintaining they were closer to the Kingdom of God than many routine believers: 'Agnostics, who are constantly exercised by the question of God, those who long for a pure heart but suffer on account of their sin, are closer to the Kingdom of God than believers whose life of faith is routine and who regard the Church merely as an institution, without letting it touch their hearts, or letting the faith touch their hearts'.

With these words, the pope was recognising that unbelievers could be authentic just as believers could be inauthentic. In Assisi, Pope Benedict XVI concluded his speech by contrasting a closed atheism, full of hostility and contempt, with an open agnosticism which seeks the truth. Agnostics of this sort, says the Pope,

> do not simply assert: 'There is no God'. They suffer from God's absence and yet are inwardly making their way towards God, inasmuch as they seek truth and goodness. They are 'pilgrims of truth, pilgrims of peace'. They ask ... militant atheists ... to leave polemics aside and to become seekers ... They also challenge the followers of religions not to consider God as their own property ... They are seeking the true God, whose image is frequently concealed in the religions because of the ways in which they are often practised ... So all their struggling and questioning is in part an appeal to believers to purify their faith.

Michael Paul was convinced that believers can fail, because they are too often tempted to see God as their possession, and to view religion as an anchor of security instead of as a source of transformation. By contrast, open and authentic agnostics seek the truth, and in doing so are seeking the true God. Indeed, some religious beliefs and some of the inadequate and unholy ways in which believers practise their faith can impede the authentic search of these agnostics. Michael Paul felt that if believers could take the honest struggles and questionings of non-believers more seriously, these questions and struggles could help them to purify their own relationship with God.

Michael Paul wanted to reach across this critical gulf of our time: the gulf between belief and unbelief, the chasm that runs through each of us. In doing so he was building upon the outreach to atheists already visible in the Second Vatican Council. When it came to the issue of the salvation of unbelievers, that council was silent about the question of culpability. Instead, in the case of genuine unbelievers, it spoke of the failure to perceive love. That failure can beset believers as well, of course, but sometimes a moment comes when the thirst for love becomes so palpable that God does as well. Douglas Coupland expressed this well in *Life After God*, words that Michael Paul often quoted:

> Now here is my secret. I tell it to you with an openness of heart that I doubt I shall ever achieve again, so I pray that you are in a quiet room as you hear these words. My secret is that I need God – that I am sick and can no longer make it alone. I need God to help me give, because I no longer seem to be capable of giving; to help me be kind, as I no longer seem capable of kindness; to help me love, as I seem beyond being able to love.

In his own ministry, Michael Paul modelled the adventurous new Catholic practice of dialoguing with unbelievers, and sharing with them in a genuine way. He was convinced that he could learn from unbelievers. He also was convinced they could teach him to respect the mystery of God. Through their unbelief, he grew to appreciate how truly mysterious and profound God must be. If they could not figure out God, how could he claim to? Thanks to them, Michael Paul could acknowledge that his ultimate response to God was not the grasp of knowledge but the humility of being grasped. He saw that paradoxically the divine mystery grows with increasing revelation. Just as we can listen again and again to the organ works of Johann Sebastian Bach, each time discovering new and unsuspected depths, so it is analogously with God. However much we receive, God's essential mystery is inexhaustible. There is always more to discover.

## Faith as a Truth of Love

Surprisingly, perhaps, unbelief is not limited to unbelievers. A completely new picture of Mother Teresa of Calcutta was revealed in 2007, with the publication of her private writings, entitled *Come Be My Light*. There we read of her decades-long experience of darkness, finding such extraordinary declarations as 'There is no God in me'. Of course, there is a crucial difference between a figure like Mother Teresa and many people in our secularised world. In the case of Mother Teresa, the emptiness is inner and spiritual in nature; in the case of many of our secularised contemporaries, it is caused by social factors, intellectual reservations or blockages of the heart. Nevertheless, the example of Mother Teresa has a universal import. It tells us that we can recover faith through staying true to the humble mystery of the everyday, through fidelity to the practice of active love as the only effective antidote to the gaping hole we feel inside.

Michael Paul also learned the lesson of active love practised so strikingly by Mother Teresa. He could readily recall the date: Friday, 6 March 1987. It was the first Friday of the month and also the first Friday of Lent that year. Sweltering in the heat of Maracaibo, Venezuela, he felt – somewhat tongue-in-cheek – that putting up with the scorching heat of this hottest of cities would be penance enough for him that year. Then, during Mass, he found himself listening to the Scripture reading for the day (*Is 58:6-7*). It is a well-known passage, where the prophet announces that the penance pleasing to God is 'to break unjust fetters, to undo the thongs of the yoke, to let the oppressed go free, and to break all yokes, to share your bread with the hungry and shelter the homeless poor, to clothe the one who is naked and not to turn your back on your own people'. These are powerful words, but what really astonished Michael Paul was the impact of the next word on him. It was a simple Spanish word, *entonces* ('then'). That word is repeated several times in the text: '*then* your light will shine like the dawn, *then* your righteousness will go before you ... *then* if you call, I will answer, here I am' (*Is 58:8-9*).

At that moment, Michael Paul discovered a new way of viewing faith. Love, he began to see, is bigger than faith and, even more importantly, love is our entry into faith. That was a revelation for him. Until then, he had thought that faith difficulties needed to be dealt with before people could live out their faith. But on that day, he realised that the key to faith does not lie in the mind. The prophet Isaiah clearly puts our commitment to the welfare of our neighbour in first place. If we take a stand against oppression, says Isaiah, and if we struggle to heal this broken world, *then* Yahweh will answer, 'I am here'. Faith is a truth of love much more than it is a truth of reason. If we live our faith first, *then* we will discover what it means. Faith is not a truth that you first try to work out in your head in theoretical fashion. Rather, the proof of faith is found in practice. The way I live my life will affect the kind of faith I have. If I put myself or some other idol at the centre of my world, God will inevitably seem far away and of little importance. It is the choices we make and put into practice that decide whether we encounter God or not.

Michael Paul was also drawn to the gentle image of love's relationship to faith that he discovered in the writings of the Swiss theologian,

Hans Urs von Balthasar (1905–88). Balthasar wrote more books than the average person reads in a lifetime, and he was a fine pianist who could play most of Mozart's works by heart. In order to illustrate what faith means, von Balthasar invites his readers to think about the first smile of an infant. It usually takes several weeks before this smile arrives, and it only happens after a mother has herself smiled over and over again at her child. And then, one day, something special happens when she receives the first smile of her child in return. That smile is confirmation that the mother has stirred up love in her child's heart, and it expresses the very shape of faith. Our faith, like the first smile of a child, is our response to a gift we have already received. Love comes first, and then faith. God radiates love, and so sparks the flame of love in our hearts in response. Just as the child responds to its mother with a smile of gratitude and trust, so faith is the recognition of a love that is already there, that already envelops us. By becoming aware of this ever-present love, we are enabled to give a wholehearted 'yes' to it.

Many people never come to the point of seeing faith as a response to a love that already surrounds us. Many people never make the connection between human love and divine love, and that includes believers as well as unbelievers. Many professed Christians picture God in such a detached and cold way that it is impossible for them to see a child's smile in response to its mother's love as an image of their relationship to God. They have no idea that human trust can teach us a lot about faith.

John Henry Cardinal Newman (1801–90), a figure Michael Paul admired greatly, attempted to deepen the Christian understanding of faith by urging his readers to reflect upon the importance of trust. 'We are acting on trust every hour of our lives', wrote Newman. He emphasised that faith is about a relationship, and so if we fail to approach faith with an open disposition, we block our access to it, whether we realise it or not. Every loving relationship entails a risk, the risk of going beyond what we can see here and now, the risk of saying a 'yes' that extends into an unseen future.

## Gravity and Grace

At each stage of our lives we can choose to say 'yes' or 'no', to ascend upwards or to descend downwards. The French philosopher and mystic, Simone Weil (1909–43), contrasts two decisive life-forces that we experience. The negative pole she calls 'gravity', a downward force that pulls us toward egoism and selfishness. The positive pole she calls 'grace', which has the marvellous capacity to suspend the laws of spiritual gravity, drawing us upward toward goodness and love.

Michael Paul found many examples in literature of the escape from egoism and self-preoccupation to the more generous horizon of love, the escape from gravity to grace. A stirring instance of this ascent is Gabriel's moment of illumination in James Joyce's short story, 'The Dead'. The noted Joycean scholar Richard Ellman remarks that 'the revelation on this night is rude to Gabriel's whole being. On this night he acknowledges that love must be a feeling which he has never fully had'. This moment of revelation takes place, fittingly, on 6 January, the Feast of the Epiphany. Gabriel and his wife Gretta return to their room in the Gresham Hotel after a party. Gabriel is taken aback when Gretta mentions that the song, 'The Lass of Aughrim', sung at the party, has brought back memories of a boy she knew when she was young. Feeling jealous, Gabriel inquires coldly about the boy at first, until the full force of the truth hits him when his wife says, 'I think he died for me'. Gabriel realises that his love for Gretta has never climbed to such sacrificial heights: 'Generous tears filled Gabriel's eyes. He had never felt like that himself towards any woman but he knew that such a feeling must be love.'

Another faith explorer whom Michael Paul admired, the Italian theologian and musician Pierangelo Sequeri (born in 1944), also highlights the significance of trust. Sequeri goes beyond Newman, by claiming that trust is such a vital element in our make-up that it is at the heart of what it means to be human. Living in an age where science prevails above all else, our notion of knowing has been reduced to something neutral, cold and dispassionate. We have lost our confidence in trust, so that we no longer 'trust' it enough. We look down upon trust as an inferior way of knowing.

Sequeri suggests that we need to reflect much more deeply on our vital capacity to trust. Only then will we be truly ready for the richness of faith. Trust places us firmly in a relationship, because we always trust another person, and by our trust we recognise that person's dignity, acknowledging that that person is worthy of our confidence. At the same time, Sequeri points out that trust isn't automatic. We struggle to trust. There is a constant inner battle between trust and mistrust, between friendliness and hostility. Even when we are not hostile, we can still be hesitant in our relationships. In so many of our normal conversations we play it safe because we're scared of being rejected and judged. We're reluctant to become more honest and so more vulnerable, because we've been scorned when we did so in the past. But sometimes when we take a courageous step, and reveal ourselves in a more real way, something new can be born, the kind of trust that changes us. That transformation through trust gives us a sense of what faith involves. Faith means going beyond our own hesitations and tentativeness in order to embark on a journey of trust.

## Finding the Key Within

Like Newman and Sequeri, Michael Paul urged people to enter into themselves, and to listen for the inner voice, the voice of God in their hearts. He was convinced that it was much easier than we imagine to get in touch with this mysterious presence and, consequently, that it was much less difficult than we think to escape from our zones of imprisonment. He liked to recall the following incident as a little parable of how relatively effortless it is to come into contact with the mystery inside us.

At the beginning of the new millennium, he was giving a summer course in New York's Fordham University, and living in a room in the Jesuit community on campus. One day he stepped into the elevator that would take him from the basement to the third floor. He pushed the '3' button, the doors closed, but the elevator didn't move. He tried again, and again nothing happened. Button '2' didn't work either. Feeling a mounting sense of panic, Michael Paul was about to press the alarm bell, but decided first to try the final button, button '4'. To his immense relief, the elevator clicked into motion and brought him to the fourth storey, from where he walked down to the floor below. Later, as he recounted this incident at dinner, his companions looked at him in surprise and said, 'Don't you have the key?' Taking out his bunch of keys, he noticed for the first time a tiny key on the keyring. It was the key he needed to gain access to the community floors. He was in possession of the key, but didn't know he had it.

Michael Paul was convinced that each of us has the key to all the floors of our humanity, but we don't realise it, and so miss out on the richness within us. The key – opening ourselves to the wonder of our own humanity – is already in our hands, however, and this in turn opens us to the larger mystery that is God. Michael Paul helped many people to go beyond their surface selves, and to become familiar with the unexplored strata inside. He showed them the key they already had.

# CHAPTER FIVE
# THE SENSE OF WONDER

A religious journey must begin with some experience of wonder; otherwise one will neither be in touch with one's deepest hungers nor able to listen to the love poem of God which is called revelation.
*Free to Believe*

A central struggle for us all is to reach the hunger and wonder at the core of each person, or as they say in the East, to get to the cave of the heart where the Spirit dwells. Or as Paul Tillich used to say, God is the name we give to an 'inexhaustible depth' within us; and any entry point to that depth is a potential road to God.
*Where is your God?*

*D*uring the years he spent teaching English literature to first-year students in University College Dublin, Michael Paul used to take a mischievous delight in writing three intriguing words on the blackboard: 'ha', 'aha' and 'ah'. He enjoyed seeing the puzzled faces of the students in the large lecture theatre before he explained their meaning. These three words, he claimed, stood for the three basic ways they could approach literature. They also pointed, he would add, to three fundamental stances they could assume towards human life in general.

'Ha' – and he would say it with great force in his best *basso profundo* voice – was suggestive of a smug, even dismissive, attitude to the material before them. He would advise his students not to fall into the trap of arriving too quickly at judgements or dismissing what they read out of hand. Instead, they should take the trouble of experiencing and understanding it properly. Coming to the second word, 'Aha', he would pronounce it in a rising tone, suggesting the moment when understanding happens and something clicks into place in the mind. He would tell them how college was meant to be full of these 'aha' moments, as they learned new things and discovered fresh insights. Then, looking solemnly at his audience and addressing them in a tone of mock gravity, Michael Paul would warn his students not to become so intoxicated by their 'aha' moments that they ended up stifling the foundational moment of it all – the experience of wonder, the 'ah' experience.

Michael Paul brought this liberating 'ah' to many Irish people – especially students and young searchers, but also to priests, religious and Church leaders – and later, through his work in Rome, to countless students from around the world. He had a disarming gift for helping people to reach the threshold of wonder in their lives. He invited them to open new doors into the mystery of themselves, so that they could discover a God who was beyond anything they had dared to imagine.

Michael Paul was convinced that some experience of wonder must accompany the beginning of the religious journey. If this doesn't happen, we fail to connect with the deepest longings within us and we also fail to see that the core of God's revelation is an encounter of love. There is frequently the temptation to judge faith in a dismissive way as nonsensical or irrelevant – the 'ha' approach – instead of experiencing it first. We rush into judgment because we wrongly presume that faith is a body of intellectual knowledge, whereas in reality it is a love story; and that is why we must begin by experiencing it. Arising from this initial experience of faith, we are usually prompted to formulate questions to help us understand our faith. This is the 'aha' spirit, and it is on the basis of this exploration that we can validly make our judgments. The journey starts, however, with 'ah'. Faith begins when we allow our hearts, and not only our reason, to be touched. As Pascal puts it, 'The heart has its reasons of which reason knows nothing'.

## The Influence of Lonergan

With these three simple words Michael Paul showed his knack for expressing difficult ideas – in this instance Bernard Lonergan's complicated theory of knowledge – in a catchy way that makes sense and is easy to remember. The thought of the Jesuit philosopher and theologian Bernard Lonergan (1904–84), although admired by many scholars, is also notoriously difficult to understand. The fact that Michael Paul was able to make it so accessible is in itself a remarkable achievement. Anyone who has delved into Lonergan's book *Insight: A Study of Human Understanding*, first published in 1953, will agree that this work of almost 800 pages is difficult and at times almost incomprehensible. It is also exhaustive – not to say exhausting – in its treatment of its subjects. For instance, in the second-last chapter, Lonergan lists various qualities of God, finally arriving after numerous closely argued pages at the following sentence, 'In the twenty-sixth place, God is personal'. By this stage, it's likely that most readers will have forgotten the previous twenty-five points!

The good news about Lonergan's thought is that, despite the often complex and abstract examples he uses, there is a relatively simple goal at the back of it all: to help people use their heads better. Lonergan was trying to introduce people to themselves, by showing them how they come to know, and how knowledge itself works. Michael Paul learned something truly important from Lonergan. He learned that knowledge is a process, a process that starts with 'ah', goes on to 'aha', and culminates in 'ha'. There is no genuine knowledge if we limit the process to only one of the three elements in it. Lonergan explained that knowing isn't just one single operation;

rather it is a series of three operations.

Lonergan also went a step further. As well as showing people how their knowing process worked, Lonergan introduced people to themselves in a deeper way, by going beneath the cognitive level, and getting them in touch with how they pictured the world, and with their feelings, moods and dispositions. In this respect, Lonergan showed that he had learned at the school of Saint Ignatius, who was deeply attuned to the contours of his inner experience, and who knew that the first step to freedom involves becoming aware of the conflicts within.

Michael Paul was drawn by this aspect in a special way. He searched for the unseen depths of people, and he brought these inner depths into the light. He tried to make sense of the inner world of others, and to help them escape their unfreedoms. He probed gently but insistently, enabling them to arrive at the 'aha' moments, when, connecting the dots in their experiences, they arrived at some kind of understanding.

Michael Paul realised that many of us are tempted to short-circuit the whole process of knowing. We think we know just by looking, and we don't take the trouble to understand. It's like the person who wakes up on a windy night, sees what is in fact a white sheet flapping on the clothesline, but takes it to be a ghost. We easily jump to facile judgments without bothering first of all to look carefully and to understand what we see.

## A Concrete Example

Richard and his fiancée Marian were both former students of Michael Paul. They decided to get married, and asked Michael Paul to officiate at their wedding. Michael Paul knew that Marian was a committed believer, but when they met to discuss the ceremony, he discovered that Richard had stopped practising his faith as a young teenager. Michael Paul invited Richard to meet him to reflect on what faith meant or didn't mean to him, and how he could participate meaningfully in the ceremony.

Over the course of a long and open conversation, Richard explained that his faith in God had collapsed when he was fourteen years of age, because everything he had been taught about God creating the world was out of touch with what he was discovering from his new passion for science. Science had ushered in a fascinating new world for him, a world that seemed to explain everything. He stopped trying to figure out religion, and made up his mind that faith was only for children. It was like outgrowing his belief in Santa Claus, he said, and just as painless. Over a period of time, he stopped going to Mass and gave up any semblance of prayer. Religion had become a complete blank for him.

Michael Paul quickly realised that the God that Richard had rejected as a young teenager was a God who was perceived like some theorem out of algebra. In the course of their conversation, he helped Richard to see that the only God who was worthy of his faith was completely different from that abstract construction. He explained that the God worth believing in is the God of Abraham, Isaac and Jacob, the God of concrete persons with concrete names, the personal God, the God of love: the God of Jesus Christ.

This was new territory for Richard, but he was now ready to explore it for the first time. Because he was in love with Marian, love itself seemed believable, and he began to see that if he was going to find God, it wouldn't be through some barren explanation of the universe. If he was going to meet God, he would do so in a personal way. He was beginning to think that he wasn't as far away from faith as he had imagined. He began to wonder about faith in a fresh way, a way that hadn't been possible when he was fourteen years old.

As they reached the end of their talk together, Michael Paul suggested something for Richard to do before their next meeting.

He invited him to open himself up to prayer.

'You want me to go back saying prayers?' asked Richard in astonishment.

'No, that's not what I am trying to say', replied Michael Paul. 'What I mean is that if you spend time wondering where you've come to now in your journey, that very wondering could bring you into contact with God, and that's a form of prayer.'

'But I haven't prayed in years', Richard exclaimed.

'I know,' said Michael Paul, 'but maybe you're not really alone in all this wondering. Just stop and try to listen for the voice of the Spirit, because I'm convinced that the Holy Spirit is at work within you. If you listen, you might find that God is actually speaking to you.'

'That would be a big step for me, after all these years away from God', said Richard.

'A lot of other people have taken a big step like that', Michael Paul assured him, adding that he felt this was the right way forward for Richard at this time.

'You might just be right', said Richard with an air of surprise at what he himself was saying. 'It never dawned on me until now that religion needs another type of listening, another sort of seeking.'

'Or maybe it's about you being sought by God', said Michael Paul with a smile.

'That would really surprise me,' said Richard, scratching his chin, 'but after this conversation, I'm beginning to believe that some crazy surprises could actually be true.'

## Listening for the Gems

During Michael Paul's years teaching English at UCD, hundreds of students – perhaps even more – dropped by his office in the Arts Building, Room J211. He was a busy man. He had lectures to prepare, books to write and many other commitments. It would have been tempting to judge these students in a 'ha' way, by groaning inwardly and thinking, 'Oh no! Here comes another bothersome student to distract me from my real work!' But Michael Paul didn't respond like that. Instead, he welcomed students, and relished the opportunity to listen to them and to their stories.

He knew it might take time for them to say what was truly in their hearts, but he was willing to wait, and even to probe, always in a gentle and respectful way. Michael Paul had the gift of being really present to others. When he listened to you, you felt that he was *all* present. He was attentive to you and to what was going on inside you. He was noticing things in you, even things you didn't notice yourself. He was asking perceptive questions that helped you get in touch with the truth inside.

When listening to people, Michael Paul had a strategy that helped him to hear what was really going on inside. That strategy meant listening for the gems. He was convinced that there was a treasure inside each person, even if it was deeply buried. That was the first assumption. The second assumption was that it was quite likely that the person concerned was unaware of this treasure. The third assumption, and the most important, was that God is always knocking on the door and never gives up. He realised that most people longed to open the door but were also afraid of doing so. A little encouragement might be all that was needed to allow God in.

Here is an example of his unique method at work. A young college student, let's call him David, came to talk to Michael Paul one day about problems he had in writing an essay. He stayed longer than he meant, because he began to talk about the problems he was having with his parents. David's home situation wasn't that bad, in fact, but a space of non-communication had opened up between his parents and himself since he had started college. There were many new things happening in David's life, including new ways of thinking about himself, and he felt his parents would never be able to understand what was going on in him. His main interest was in 'finding himself', while his parents were intent on his doing well and getting a good job.

The major breakthrough in the conversation between David and Michael Paul came when they both realised that David had never spoken to anyone in this new language of self-discovery. It sounded new even to David himself. As Michael Paul continued to listen, he became aware of the great goodness inside David. He also came to realise that the goodness was eclipsed by clouds of self-doubt, feelings of guilt and shadows of confusion. So at one point in their conversation, Michael Paul suddenly said, 'Break the magnifying glass and throw it away'.

Seeing that David was puzzled by this intervention, Michael Paul opened the page of a book and asked David to imagine what it would look like if a magnifying glass were held over the middle of the page. After a certain amount of coaxing, David ventured to say that certain words would probably appear much larger, while at the same time everything else would be distorted. Michael Paul explained that David was like someone with a large magnifying glass, making the few difficulties in his life stand out in a way that obscured the bigger story of who he was. That made sense to David, and it enabled him to begin putting his concerns in context and to see the whole picture.

Before the whole picture could emerge, however, it was necessary for David to pluck up the courage to express the negative concerns he had. His honesty about his disappointments actually made way for a new sense of hope. For a long time, those hurts had been bottled up in a resentful silence, occupying the whole page and distorting everything else. Once David found the opportunity of expressing these disappointments gently and in a trusting atmosphere, the goodness inside, which until then had been hidden under all that numbness, became more and more visible.

When supervising the research of doctoral students at the Gregorian University, Michael Paul operated in a similar manner. He used to encourage them to discover their particular question, and then – once they had found it – to devote their energy to answering it. Implicit in this advice was a deep trust in his students; he truly believed that they had a hidden treasure inside. Often the treasure was scattered in different places, and they had to rummage around to find the various pieces and bring them together. But once they had extracted their particular question out of the often confusing thread of their lives, once they had unearthed the question that really fired them, he encouraged them to trust it and to follow it.

Bernard Lonergan also underlined the importance of questions. He reflected upon that familiar phase in childhood when children can't stop asking questions, often pestering their parents for answers. They ask endlessly 'What is that?' and 'What is it for?' and when they get an answer they pass on to a further, even more searching, question, 'Why?' Lonergan identified this drive to ask questions as a drive that is basic to all human beings. We're all curious in one way or another, and we all want to know and to understand. We all have questions, many of them deep questions.

## The Rehabilitation of Wonder

Michael Paul was profoundly interested in people, and that's why he enjoyed the adventure of encountering so many students. He found himself naturally wondering about the mystery inside them, and he tried to help them identify and cherish their own inner landscape. Above all, through his life and his thought, Michael Paul rehabilitated wonder in the context of faith. If we explore this facet of Michael Paul, it may just bring us closer to the heart of his thinking.

First, it is worth our while to ask about the nature of wonder. Dictionaries usually define it in terms such as the following: 'Wonder is a feeling of surprise, curiosity, and even amazement, admiration and awe, caused by something unusual, strange, beautiful or remarkable'. Wonder, then, is a feeling and an emotion. It is not any kind of emotion, but a positive emotion. It doesn't emerge from a vacuum; instead it is a response to something that catches us off guard, something surprising and unexpected, something that stops us in our tracks, and which doesn't quite fit into our habitual way of looking at things. Wonder has an element of mystery about it, but it is not experienced as problematic.

In this context, the distinction between 'problem' and 'mystery' given by the French philosopher Gabriel Marcel can be helpful. According to Marcel, a problem is something we can stand back from and look at in a detached way. This is the way faith has frequently been explored in fundamental theology, which was Michael Paul's discipline in Rome. In an effort to demonstrate the credibility of some aspect of faith, its doctrinal content was examined and elaborated as a set of abstract truths to be understood and explained. Michael Paul realised more than most that such an approach is unlikely to appeal to the deep hungers of our contemporaries. Who wants to pray to an Unmoved Mover, a First Cause or a Necessary Being? As Martin Heidegger once remarked, 'Before the *causa sui*, man can neither fall to his knees in awe nor can he play music and dance before this god'.

While a problem is something to be viewed with a cold and dispassionate eye, a mystery invites personal involvement. Michael Paul was always struck by the challenge facing believers to hold on to faith in a culture that questions it so much. Their most urgent need, he believed, is *not* to stand back from faith and analyse it with the help of complicated abstract arguments. For this reason, the most important way to assist them is *not* through scholastic arguments or doctrinal statements. Instead, they need help to see that deep within them, even if somewhat obscured, there is something astonishing and wonderful, something we call the soul.

## Discovering the Soul

*The Catechism of the Catholic Church* calls the soul the 'innermost aspect ... that which is of greatest value', the part of us by which we are 'most especially in God's image'. Michael Paul believed that, if people could only get in touch with this reality, the rest would follow. The mystery of God speaks to us from within, he believed, and the best way to find God is to get in touch with the deepest core of ourselves. The ideal preparation for encountering God himself is to become aware of the reflected goodness of God planted within.

Michael Paul was deeply aware of the enormous amount of hurt and pain many people have to endure in their lives. He knew well, through hours of listening, the struggles and anxieties that burden so many people's lives. Nevertheless, he believed that everyone was drawn by the presence of the soul, even if darkness and 'self-clouds' had eclipsed it so that only a tiny sliver of its brilliant radiance was visible. In his gentle yet insistent way, he lobbied for an enlargement of fundamental theology beyond the question of the credibility of faith to the question of its 'liveability'. His principal concern was not to convince people of the truth of faith, but instead to show them that it was possible to incarnate faith in their lives by opening their eyes to the world of wonder within, where God was already touching them and they were in touch with God.

Wonder has the capacity to open us up to something beyond ourselves, because its source is from beyond us. The initiative for this opening up comes from beyond us as well; something from outside reaches out and touches us, surprising and even overwhelming us. Wonder is similar to grace, in the sense that it is gratuitous, free, unmerited, unearned and undeserved.

There is a memorable line in *Antigone*, the ancient Greek tragedy by Sophocles: 'Wonders are many, and none is more wonderful than man.' Wonder invites us to burst into song. What made Michael Paul burst into song? I don't recall him ever becoming especially animated at seeing blood-red sunsets or copper beech trees or snow-capped mountains. I seldom heard him describing the astonishing vistas he must have seen on his many travels abroad. Unlike Seamus Heaney and many other Irish thinkers and writers, he didn't seem to experience huge wonder at the landscape or have a visceral bond with the land. Michael Paul's wonder was aroused above all by something he couldn't immediately see. In line with Bernard Lonergan's insistence that knowing is more than taking a look, Michael Paul was immediately drawn by the invisible element in people, by that indefinable quality, by the soul. As he made clear in the imaginary letter he wrote to St Ignatius, quoted in Chapter One above, Michael Paul had learned to make his own Ignatius's passion for 'helping souls'.

Michael Paul wanted people to get in touch with their souls, but that didn't mean that God and faith would necessarily be introduced in the early stages of a conversation, as illustrated by this revealing story. A young priest came to Michael Paul on one occasion to ask his advice. The priest was hoping to get through to the young people in his parish. He had worked hard at putting together some material on themes from the *Catechism of the Catholic Church* which he hoped would appeal to them. To his great disappointment, the attendance quickly fell off and they soon stopped coming altogether. He asked Michael Paul for his advice.

Michael Paul reply was typical: 'Back up a little bit'. He explained that many of our deep hungers are human hungers, and we have to begin with these. The journey of these young people had not yet brought them to the point of openness the priest was expecting. They needed help to find their own questions before they would be open to the wisdom emanating from the Christian tradition. They needed to pay attention to their own experience and discover their own depth before they would be ready to appreciate the depth of their faith.

They needed help to go beyond the suffocating spaces of their lives in order to cultivate a disposition of wonder. With the right disposition, a space of listening can be opened where, as Newman said, 'heart speaks to heart'.

## Growing in Reverence

Michael Paul's sense of wonder meant he had a reverent way of thinking about others and approaching others. This sense of reverence is what Blaise Pascal describes as the *esprit de finesse*. Pascal makes an illuminating distinction between the *esprit de géométrie* (spirit of geometry) and the *esprit de finesse* (spirit of finesse). The *esprit de géométrie* is reason in its calculating, instrumental, analytic and scientific mode, the kind of reasoning that, despite its many positive aspects, at the same time dominates and exploits nature. The *esprit de géométrie* does not have an attitude of respect before reality; instead, it refashions the world as we human beings decide the world ought to be. The *esprit de finesse* is reason in a more reverent, refined and gentle mode. It is reason as gracious and as graced, as rooted in the heart. It is tender and compassionate. It doesn't reduce people to things or to objects. It respects and cherishes their uniqueness. It doesn't have the rigidity and inflexibility you find in the *esprit de géométrie*. The *esprit de géométrie* versus the *esprit de finesse* is power versus tenderness. We need both, but the *esprit de géométrie* seems to have expanded to preposterous proportions over the last few hundred years in the Western world, while the *esprit de finesse* has been greatly neglected, largely because it doesn't make money or lead to personal glory.

These two contrasting spirits are not only out there in society; they are also inside each heart. We can be gracious and respectful, but we can also be judgmental and condemning. These attitudes affect our images of God, which can sometimes be totally unworthy of him. If we are to grow in faith, Michael Paul realised, we need simultaneously to purify our distorted images of God. Many of these images emerge when the impressionable imagination of childhood runs up against a threatening use of religion. A naughty child may be told, for example, 'You can't fool God, because he knows everything'. A menacing remark like that can disturb a young child, and root itself so indelibly in the memory that it is almost impossible to erase, even by years of solid religious education.

How did Michael Paul deal with these false images of God? Rather than fighting them directly or trying to demolish them by argument, he instead used his conversational gifts to reveal another God. He made it clear that he didn't believe in those false gods either. On the positive side, he introduced people to the gospels, to the person of Jesus Christ and to the God he proclaims as Father. Above all, he encouraged them to try the most healing way of all – prayer – and so to have a direct encounter with God.

Although Michael Paul composed that beautiful poem 'Monique in Caen', and a few other poems of his have survived, he did not himself become a poet. But he had that gift that all the best poets possess: the ability to enter imaginatively into the experience of others. Returning to those three memorable words – 'ha', 'aha', and 'ah' – it's worth noting that in order to enter in a sympathetic way into the experience of others, we need to suspend judgment, and leave aside the 'ha' moment. We also need to distance ourselves temporarily from our own 'aha' dimension – from our own way of understanding things. To the extent that we can do that, we will be able to step into the other person's shoes and see the world through the eyes of the other. We will be able to arrive at their 'ah' level and perhaps, like Michael Paul, liberate their human depths.

# CHAPTER SIX
# IMAGINATION

The real battles of life take place within the human imagination (as Cardinal Newman argued over a century ago). How do we see ourselves? What do we hope for? What is it all about? The deeper answers, whether positive or negative, are found in how we imagine our lives, not just in how we think about them. It is on that level that we find either anchors of wisdom or else suffer from dispersion and emptiness.
*Dive Deeper*

Human imagination is the space where faith is either starved or nourished. The American poet Emily Dickinson expressed it with typical concision: 'The possible's slow fuse is lit by imagination'. In colder words imagination is our faculty of possibility, and if God is the greatest of possibilities, the light of faith needs to explode (Dickinson's metaphor) not in our minds but in our imaginations. *Into Extra Time*

*M*ichael Paul was so enlivened by his sabbatical year in Latin America (1986 7) that for some years afterwards he was hoping to return to teach theology in Paraguay and to help in the formation of young Jesuits there. The intended move to Paraguay never transpired. Because of his research and writings on unbelief, he was invited in 1990 to work in the Vatican instead, where he spent five years serving in the Pontifical Council for Dialogue with Non-Believers, which was subsequently assimilated into the Pontifical Council for Culture. He brought his usual enthusiasm and creativity to this task, but he missed the stimulation of university life, with the energy, challenges and new perspectives which the students brought. It was something of a relief for him, therefore, when he was appointed in 1995 to teach theology in the Pontifical Gregorian University in Rome.

## The Roman Phase

In addition to his role as lecturer at the Gregorian University, Michael Paul was later appointed Dean of Theology there and also Rector of the Collegio Bellarmino, residence of a large community of Jesuit graduate students. Despite his teaching load and the heavy burden of administration, he somehow found time to write, give talks and listen to many young searchers, helping them to enter into a space of freedom they often did not know they had. In terms of his own writing, he began to see himself more and more as having the gift of translating the insights of major theologians into a language that educated but non-specialist readers could understand. He liked to use the French phrase *haute vulgarisation* for this endeavour. The phrase does not suggest mere popularisation, but something more demanding: the spreading of knowledge aimed at rendering the original as perfectly and faithfully as possible.

If he were playing in a rock band, Michael Paul's instrument would undoubtedly be the synthesiser! In his writings, he learned from many different literary and theological sources, and brought forth something fresh as a result. The distinguished American biologist Edward O. Wilson has pinpointed the contemporary need for synthesisers: 'We are drowning in information, while starving for wisdom. The world henceforth will be run by synthesisers – people able to put together the right information at the right time, think critically about it, and make important choices wisely.' Michael Paul liked putting ideas together in ways that others could understand. He had a creative mind that asked unexpected questions and came up with fresh approaches. He had a reverent mind, which didn't condemn those who were different from him. He had an ethical mind, which acknowledged that ideas have consequences and that we bear responsibility for how we think and live. He also had a disciplined mind, because he had learned about the process of knowledge from Bernard Lonergan.

## The Power of Imagination

With his lively imagination, Michael Paul was able to visualise culture in various striking ways. In one image, he talks of culture as an ocean in which we swim like fish. We are immersed daily in a flood of images from TV, internet and mass media, some of which help us to grow, whilst others stunt our development by offering us false and damaging pictures of the world. In another image, he compares culture to a lens through which we gaze, not realising that there are other ways of seeing. In a related image, he compares culture to a pair of darkened spectacles which blind us to the fact that there are more illuminating ways of viewing reality. Culture is like the air we breathe, and that air can be healthy or polluted, or more probably both; it helps us breathe, but can also suffocate us. After a while we may not even notice that we are choking. Culture, in another image, is a filter that allows certain images of reality to come into our consciousness, and excludes others. Our families, experiences, education, beliefs and customs all influence what we see and how we see it.

Most striking, perhaps, Michael Paul envisages culture as both a prison cell and a zone of freedom. Western culture, in particular, has furnished the prison with so many wonderful gadgets that we imagine we are actually living it up in a luxury hotel. It is a five-star prison from which few of us even want to escape. How do we get out of this prison? According to Michael Paul, we must become aware of our hunger for something bigger and better than a comfortable but claustrophobic life; we must be humble enough to admit that there are dimensions of reality that surpass us; and we must pursue this larger reality that we cannot understand or even contain. In the process we need to enlarge our imagination.

Imagination, for Michael Paul, means not just the ability to produce concrete images of things that are abstract, but the ability to dream up new possibilities, to come up with connections between seemingly disconnected things, and to articulate an original vision or outlook on life. His book *Dive Deeper: the Human Poetry of Faith* (2001) is a superb example of his imaginative ability to make believable connections between people who to all appearances are quite disconnected. He sets up a series of imaginary conversations between disparate figures: Jane Austen speaks to D. H. Lawrence about relationships; Flannery O'Connor talks with George Eliot about human vulnerability; William Shakespeare and Oscar Romero converse about suffering; Rainer Maria Rilke muses with Karl Rahner about the immense sea of mystery and the hidden river of ordinary life; and – most intriguingly of all – sparks of difference and a flame of understanding shoot up between Thérèse of Lisieux and Friedrich Nietzsche as they share their insights into some of the deepest questions of human existence. In the final exchange of the book, a contemporary searcher called 'The Self' comes into contact with Christ himself.

## Imaginative approaches

Michael Paul's imaginative streak is already evident in his first book, *Help my Unbelief*. In it he anticipates many of the themes he would develop over the coming forty years. Its most arresting moment comes in its very opening line: 'It was a Thursday evening at Mass that I entered my atheism in a deeper way than ever before'. Michael Paul was referring to a temporary bout of atheism he experienced, where he felt overcome by doubts, wanting to believe but unable to do so, until the moment he received communion. This bout of unbelief made him understand that faith was a more astounding gift than he had ever fathomed, and it left him 'with a sense both of the strangeness of faith always and of its special fragility today'.

The book is divided into three sections. In the first part, he creates an imaginary dialogue on the future of faith between a quartet of believers. He deliberately gives them names from the New Testament, suggesting that their different viewpoints on the situation of faith in today's world reflect diverging approaches already evident in figures from Scripture. Peter, a busy priest in a parish, echoes his namesake in his pastoral concern for his flock and his cautious leadership. He is the defender of the institution. Paul, a priest in youth ministry, reflects the New Testament Paul in his emphasis on evangelising and on the way faith affects the person. James, a social worker in the inner city, mirroring the New Testament author of the same name, is a liberation theologian, proclaiming that faith without works is empty. Martha is a wife and mother of four who, like the woman in the gospel story, is taken up by the practical demands of keeping a household together. At the end of their lengthy conversation, they arrive at a certain degree of convergence, despite their differences, and agree that their diversity is not only beneficial but vital, because unity does not mean uniformity.

In the second part of the book, taking his cue from C. S. Lewis's *The Screwtape Letters*, Michael Paul imagines a speech delivered by a senior demon to a group of young demons charged with undermining the Irish clergy. The instructor orders them to do their best to make priests ignore the crisis of faith in Ireland, so that they are caught out by the 'slow surprise' of what happens. 'Work on their worries in order to keep them merely negative', he insists. He picks out three strategies to intensify this negativity: fear, anger and despair. Speaking of fear, he advises the young demons to 'let their fears keep them locked within their older patterns of work and of relationships. This will lead the older men to abdicate the youth field (even though they could be excellent agents of the Enemy if their confidence held)'. In order to fuel a sense of despair among priests, the demonic instructor tells his charges to make them feel isolated from God and from one another, because 'isolation allows us to distort their reading of reality, or insinuate that they are getting nowhere and nobody appreciates their efforts'. At all costs, he orders them to keep priests stuck in an old-fashioned way of viewing their role, so that they do not dream of introducing people to a personal relationship with Jesus Christ.

In the final part of the book, Michael Paul pens imaginary letters to various people affected by the changes in faith. After writing to parents, he then goes on to address an 'in-between' person, meaning someone who has not opted out of religious practice completely, but who is in an 'undernourished limbo' with only 'outer convention and a lack of inner conviction'. The third letter is to a Church-atheist – someone who has rejected the Church but not God – and the final letter addresses an atheist friend.

The imaginative vein continues through his various works. *Free to Believe* (1987) begins with a letter to himself that perhaps reflects a 'self-atheism': his tendency to doubt himself as a writer and to want to throw in the towel. 'You will become stuck many times as you draft these pages. You will lose faith in what you set out to do. But you will also escape from prisons of unfaith again and again, so that the experience of writing this book will not be far from its central concerns: the continual battle for freedom; the constant quest for what is right; the discovery that everything can be rooted in love.' *Letters on Prayer* (1994) is made up of eighteen letters that try to do justice to the double role of prayer – giving us a new relationship with God and sending us on a mission into the heart of the world. In *Faith Maps* (2010), Michael Paul explores the thought of ten major religious thinkers, among them some less well-known figures. He concludes eight of the chapters with an imaginary monologue, as if one of these figures were speaking to us today. In all of these works, his literary background enabled Michael Paul to find creative and effective ways to communicate with his readers, weaving the wisdom of figures from the past into the fabric of contemporary issues.

## Ignatian Influence

It was not just Michael Paul's background in literature, however, that gave rise to this imaginative approach. His gifts were further honed by his experience of the imaginative prayer involved in Ignatian contemplation. St Ignatius famously, in his *Spiritual Exercises*, gave form and structure to a kind of prayer that involves placing ourselves in a scene from the Bible with the help of the imagination. He invites us to use all our senses to make this scene as real as possible: observing the look on Jesus' face, for example, and the expressions of those around him. We are to listen to the words of Jesus and to the responses of those he encounters. We are to feel the gentle breeze and catch the scent of the nearby olive tree. All the while, we are to notice our feelings and reactions as we take everything in. Most importantly, we absorb what God is saying to us personally through all of this. This kind of prayer undoubtedly deepened and broadened Michael Paul's own imaginative gifts.

Imagination for Michael Paul points beyond itself, because it also embraces a sense of wonder. It includes the capacity to discover, value and cherish things that reveal mystery, that connect us to the depth of our own humanity, and that point us toward God. Like an arctic exploration discovering, beneath the visible iceberg, the far greater mass hidden underwater, Michael Paul's notion of the imagination is ultimately an invitation to 'dive deeper'. The invitation penetrates the veil separating the visible from the invisible. Imagination leads us to a vision of something we cannot see, but which is mysteriously present.

For Michael Paul, the authentic imagination is not some kind of make-believe, enchanted by unreality. Instead, the imagination helps us to see into reality itself in a deeper way. This doesn't happen easily or without struggle, however. The false self is an onion with many layers; to arrive at the reality of who I truly am can take a lot of peeling, even a lifetime of pruning and shredding.

It's challenging to picture terminal illness, and it's even more difficult to visualise it in a way that gives hope. That's why the 'Cancer Diary' section of Michael Paul's final book, *Into Extra Time*, is extremely moving. Amidst all the anxiety and suffering, it conveys Christ's gentle presence like a background flame that can never be extinguished. Authentic imagination isn't an instrument to help us escape from the real world into some realm with no basis in reality; it isn't a pretext for fleeing the sphere of time and entering timelessness; it isn't an excuse to ascend into some ethereal orbit. True to the richness of the Christian imagination, Michael Paul reaffirmed during his illness that the imagination is something that helps us cope with the here-and-now, by enlarging our vision and our acceptance of what is unfolding. His vision was expansive enough to know that he wasn't alone in this suffering. Here's something he wrote exactly a month before he died:

> It's so simple, I'm surprised I didn't see it. When I am cast down by low energy or difficulties to face in silence, instead of resenting some spiritual intensity that is not possible, I embrace this weakness as a strange gift. I recognise now that it was a temptation to remain cast down instead of seeing my tiny and slower passion sharing in his great Passion. I was inclined to turn in on myself in spiritual impotence, when a quieter attention seemed out of reach.

## Other Influences

The role of the imagination was an abiding concern for Michael Paul. It was also a topic that engaged the interest of his professors, colleagues and friends, as well as the authors he read. As mentioned already, his supervisor in Oxford, Dame Helen Gardner, wrote a book called *In Defence of the Imagination*. A colleague in UCD, Denis Donoghue, the chair of the Department of English until he moved to New York University, wrote a literary study of the imagination, *The Sovereign Ghost*, which Michael Paul was to review favourably. His good friend William F. Lynch SJ wrote a series of books on images and the imagination. The New York-based Michael Warren, who has written extensively on youth ministry, has also highlighted the importance of the imagination. In the philosophy of the French thinker Paul Ricoeur, Michael Paul found a parallel with what he had discovered in St Ignatius: imagination as a prophetic call that invites us into a promising future surpassing our present horizons. The Canadian philosopher Charles Taylor provided him with an interesting angle on the social dimension of the imagination.

A few words about the imagination in each of these thinkers will throw light on Michael Paul's understanding of the term. First, let's turn to Helen Gardner. Speaking of Dickens's character David Copperfield and of the poet John Keats, who both used literature as a way of escaping from the difficulties of existence, Helen Gardner comments in *In Defence of the Imagination*, 'I do not regard this as a sign of weakness, a refusal to face life. On the contrary, I regard it as a sign of the resilience of their spirits, which are able to break out of the prison of the self, and refuse to be bounded by their own present wretchedness.' Michael Paul would have warmed to this idea of escaping 'the prison of the self'. As a child he was enthralled by escape stories, as we have noted. He was just six years old when the Second World War ended, and in the years that followed, there was an abundance of such stories. In fact, taking a cue from his childhood passion for these tales, Michael Paul explored the whole journey of life as an escape story in one of his books – his own personal favourite – *Free to Believe*. He argues in that book that in order to break free of the false self, we first need to recognise the battlefield within us. He suggests that we can achieve this recognition with the help of the imagination, and in particular through awareness of two kinds of images of ourselves: on the one hand, images that keep us imprisoned in the past; on the other hand, those that free in us a new sense of ourselves and of what we can be.

In 1978, Michael Paul reviewed *The Sovereign Ghost* by his colleague, the literary critic Denis Donoghue, for the Irish Jesuit quarterly, *Studies*. In this review, Michael Paul observed, 'Professor Donoghue acknowledges in more than one aside that he takes imagination as a secular term for "soul" and that it is "divine in its origins", even though we now feel safer in discerning its effects rather than its source'. Like Donoghue, Michael Paul saw the connection between the imagination and the soul, as the place where our wondering begins, where our relationships with others start, and indeed as the very source of our loving. He believed that if we could come to recognise this fathomless entity called the soul, we would in turn come to recognise God. The soul reveals the image and likeness of God in us, and precisely because it reveals the image of *God*, it is also mysterious.

In T. S. Eliot's poem 'The Love Song of J. Alfred Prufrock', Prufrock groans about 'the eyes that will fix you in a formulated phrase'. The truth is that the soul cannot be set down in a neat or tidy phrase, because it reflects the infinite richness of God. Our knowledge of the soul will always be patchy and fragmented, because of the infinite fullness of God, whose nature it reflects. Indeed, the ability to notice the soul does not arise from ourselves but is God's gift. We cannot grasp it with our intellects, but we can be grasped by it in a spirit of wonder and reverence. The more we discover it, the more we realise we cannot exhaust its mystery. The novelist Gabriel García Márquez was once asked by a friend what he thought of his wife, Mercedes, to whom he had been married for decades. Márquez replied, 'I know her so well now, that I have not the slightest idea who she is'.

The depths of the soul cannot be plumbed by scientific observation or impartial analysis, and for that reason the soul remains essentially mysterious. But its mystery can illuminate us if we find a way to wake up to its reality, so that we can in turn be awakened by the God in whose image and likeness it is fashioned. Because the soul is not only the source of wonder but also of love, the best way to strengthen it is through love. Michael Paul expressed this eloquently in *Dive Deeper*: 'God is love, not passive but flowing, energising, transforming. Like a work of beauty to the power of infinity. Like ourselves at our full range of wonder and of giving, and yet beyond all our imagining.'

Perhaps Michael Paul's favourite description of the imagination was given by his friend and fellow Jesuit, Fr William F. Lynch SJ (1908–87), who argued in his book *Christ and Prometheus* that the imagination is holistic. It is our complete self, not just one or other aspect of ourselves, he claimed.

> The imagination is not an aesthetic faculty. It is not a single or special faculty. It is all the resources of man, all his faculties, his whole history, his whole life, and his whole heritage brought to bear upon the concrete world inside and outside of himself, to form images of the world, and thus to find it, cope with it, shape it, even make it. The task of the imagination is to imagine the real … The religious imagination … tries literally to imagine things with God … The imagination is really the only way we have of handling the world.

William Lynch argued that the imagination is not just something for artists and poets; the imagination is for everyone. The imagination is not there to help us escape reality; it is there to help us deal with reality. The imagination helps us to cope with reality by showing us possibilities that aren't readily evident. It sees beyond the here-and-now.

Michael Paul had a gift for giving people a new sense of hope, and his generous imagination played a big part in this. William Lynch himself wrote an exceptional book on the connection between imagination and hope, *Images of Hope*. A basic aspect of hope is that it helps us take the next step. We live by hope, because everything we do in our daily lives, starting with getting up each morning, is grounded in the hope that what we do will move us forward in some way. The imagination also helps us move forward by enlarging our notion of what's possible. Lynch describes this persuasively:

> Imagination, if it is in prison and has tried every exit, does not panic or move into apathy but sits down to try to envision another way out. It is always slow to admit that all the facts are in, that all the doors have been tried, and that it is defeated. It is not so much that it has vision as that it is able to wait, to wait for a moment of vision which is not yet there, for a door that is not yet locked. It is not overcome by the absoluteness of the present moment.

Lynch provides an example of this liberating imagination at work from the eminent American psychiatrist, Harry Stack Sullivan. When he was faced by a patient who felt devastated by some particular incident that had recently occurred, Sullivan didn't immediately write out a prescription for medication and send his client away. Instead he asked his patient a deceptively simple question, 'When did this happen?' Now, if you have to pinpoint the moment something unpleasant happened, this also reminds you of the time before it happened, a time that wasn't so unpleasant. And so, by having to place this difficult moment in the context of a longer stretch of time, the testing moment loses its absolute quality, and becomes less overpowering. The imagination has found a way to get beyond the 'prison' of the moment and to escape the shackles of that particular incident.

If we stop to reflect, we'll realise that we all experience this healing role of the imagination. For instance, if someone asks you today to say what was really upsetting you three weeks ago, in most cases you won't be able to remember, or if you do, it will be only after an effort. Your imagination, with the help of the passage of time, has come to your rescue, not by pretending that you were never upset, but by placing that trying moment within the larger context of the last three weeks, so that it is no longer so overwhelming.

Lynch emphasises that the imagination has the patience 'to wait for a moment of vision which is not yet there'. This patient waiting implies a contemplative stance towards life, because a patient gaze is essential for contemplatives. They don't impose themselves in their seeing. Their gaze is receptive, because they allow things to be. That doesn't mean being passive, however; it means being attentive in an open, disciplined and welcoming way. A contemplative stance is really a stance of wonder.

Michael Paul was saddened by the fact that so many of us have become disconnected from wonder. We easily get embroiled in heady debates, attacking each other's ideas and shouting down the other's arguments. In the process, we lose sight of the fact that our lives are largely dominated by the images we have. He drew from the research of Michael Warren, who points out that as the imagination's role in Catholicism began to diminish, marketing experts were, ironically, spending more and more energy and money influencing the imagination of potential consumers. Advertising executives realised much better than Church leaders the truth of Cardinal Newman's maxim that 'the heart is commonly reached, not through the reason, but through the imagination'.

Warren also finds it ironical that although our society is pervaded by visual images, few of us give this fact much thought. Meanwhile, our culture actually imagines the lives of young people for them. Television, film and the internet all vividly portray the kind of life that young people are expected to pursue, and that life is frequently far removed from what Jesus proposes for them. The problem goes even deeper, however, since all those who work with youth – parents, teachers, pastors and youth ministers – are themselves being shaped by this same visual and virtual culture. If those who are concerned with youth are themselves unaware of this pervasive influence, they are most unlikely to be able to help young people to weather the onslaught that materialises daily on their mobile phones and laptops, where lessons about sexuality, family, money and life itself are being constantly communicated.

Michael Warren identifies the encounter between Jesus and the rich young man (*Mk 10:17-22*) as a decisive passage for all young people. Here 'Jesus re-imagined his life for him', showing the young man how the he could divest himself of his riches and connect himself with something deeper and more authentic. Jesus offered the rich young man a new image of himself which ran completely against the self-image his wealth had given him. Michael Warren's acute analysis invites us to ask, as Michael Paul did, some thought-provoking questions. Are we happy to allow consumerist culture kidnap our imagination? Who do we trust to imagine our lives for us?

Michael Paul was inspired by Paul Ricoeur's rich notion of the imagination as a gift that opens up new ways of living for us, new ways of re-imagining our lives. At the end of his article, 'Metaphor and the Central Problem of Hermeneutics', Ricoeur asks a searching rhetorical question: 'Are we not ready to recognise in the power of the imagination, no longer simply the faculty of deriving "images" from our sensory experience, but the capacity for letting new worlds shape our understanding of ourselves?' In a manner that evokes St Ignatius's liberating experience of the imagination on his sickbed in Loyola, Ricoeur shows how imagination challenges our jaded way of being by constantly ushering in new dreams and fresh possibilities. Like Ricoeur, Michael Paul valued the imagination as a way of opening doors, doors – as William Lynch remarks – that have not been tried, doors to seeing the world and God in a new way.

Given his great regard for the imagination, it's not surprising that Michael Paul was particularly attentive to what the Montreal-born philosopher Charles Taylor calls 'the social imaginary'. By that term is meant the intuitive way we understand ourselves in Western society, an understanding that is not spelled out in a theoretical way, but expressed implicitly in the images and stories that prevail in our societies. For instance, while the predominant picture we have of ourselves in Western culture is that of the relatively isolated individual, that is by no means the only way of perceiving ourselves. Archbishop Desmond Tutu describes a refreshingly different, African way of visualising ourselves. He uses the resonant word *ubuntu* to convey 'the fact that my humanity is caught up and is inextricably bound up in yours. I am human because I belong'. The social imaginary can have a powerful effect on our lives, keeping important realities out of sight. Because there are so many glamorous and appealing images constantly filling our minds and hearts in the Western world, God is easily excluded from the picture and we don't even realise he is not there.

*Imagination and Beauty*

If we are to begin to heal both our individual and social imaginations, we need to cultivate images that speak of ourselves as relational. Von Balthasar's image of the child's first smile, which we reflected on in Chapter Four, is not an image of an isolated individual living in a kind of vacuum, but of a vibrant relationship and loving encounter between two persons: mother and child. Our imaginations need to be fed on images of this kind if we are to be open to the reality of God in our world.

Indeed, von Balthasar recognised that our imaginations are ultimately healed by the encounter with beauty, whether it is the beauty of a mother's smile or the beauty of God's love. In the first volume of *The Glory of the Lord*, he describes the stark consequences of the banishment of beauty:

> In a world without beauty ... the good must also lose its attractiveness, the self-evidence of why it must be carried out. The human being stands before the good and asks why it must be done ... In a world that no longer has enough confidence in itself to affirm the beautiful, the proofs of the truth have lost their cogency. In other words, syllogisms may still dutifully clatter away like rotary presses or computers which infallibly spew out an exact number of answers by the minute. But the logic of these answers is itself a mechanism which no longer captivates anyone. The very conclusions are no longer conclusive.

# CHAPTER SEVEN
# FREEDOM

In ordinary existence, the danger is that happiness can sink into the trivial, that the heart can rest content with the second-rate, and above all that the invitation to grow in options of self-giving can be avoided. But life seldom allows a person to stay asleep in this way. Sooner or later something will jolt the drifter out of his or her slumber. What are these moments of awakening? The American novelist Saul Bellow has expressed it wittily through the main character in *The Adventures of Augie March*: there are, he says, two great awakeners of the spirit from its sleep, love and suffering. And he adds: love can do it, but suffering is sure.
**What Will Give Us Happiness?**

Again and again I have been told that I had a capacity to heal people's hope. This was often true in one to one meetings, in spiritual direction, in meeting students, in encounters with younger Jesuits and so on. I can recall many occasions in Rome when I would bring someone to the door after a conversation, and on the way back to my room I would sometimes drop into the chapel to say to the Lord: 'We did that well together, thank you'. It was the opposite of self-satisfaction. Rather it was a sense of humble reverence, knowing my humanity as the channel of the Spirit's artistry. **Into Extra Time**

reedom is a concern that weaves its expansive way through all of Michael Paul's writings. It is also a recurrent theme in his life, from the young child whose passion was escape stories to the dying cancer patient resonating with the Pauline hunch that when he was weak, then he was also strong.

## The Struggle for Freedom

To a certain extent we're already free, but at the same time we're not as free as we can be. Becoming free to love more fully doesn't happen automatically; it's a struggle to ready ourselves to receive the gift of freedom. And although we lack freedom in various ways, we can be blasé about it, and so our faith becomes stunted. Freedom is fragile and is easily threatened. For instance, if we lead frenetic lives and have little time to nourish our souls through periods of quiet and prayer, our lives will shrink and our faith will weaken. If we get hurt in relationships, the resulting wounds can make it more difficult for us to trust others, and also to trust God. If we live too much in our heads, it will be hard for us to get in touch with the hunger in our hearts. If we take what others do as the norm for our own lives, God will become distant and irrelevant. In challenging moments like these it doesn't make sense to spend our energy and time speculating about the meaning of faith while we neglect to look at our lack of freedom. We have to come back to where the problem is, to our struggle for freedom.

Michael Paul was convinced that growth in our own freedom marks the beginning of faith. We must become free of our surface selves in order to reach the threshold where we can hear God's voice. Over the years, Michael Paul had many conversations with students about faith, but as long as faith remained a problem that was removed from their daily living these conversations, he believed, lacked reality. He often startled them by suddenly changing the direction of their conversations and saying, 'It's not God I want to talk about, but you'. This statement was based on his intuition that before we can truly reach out to God, we need to get in touch with ourselves, with our heart-space. We cannot start from intellectual questions; we need to get in touch with our own lived struggles first. This means becoming aware of the inner tug-of-war between the superficial and the real self. It can take time for the superficial self to quieten down, of course, and Michael Paul had the wisdom and patience to give ample time to those he met for that to happen.

It was, he said, a bit like trying to enter into prayer. One of Michael Paul's students once asked him how he was able to pray. He surprised her by responding that he had little difficulty in prayer itself, but that bringing himself to prayer's threshold was something he found hard. Drawing on his Indian experience, he told her that the tree of his mind was so full of monkeys that kept chattering and jumping from one branch to another that he needed a lot of patience with himself in order to still their incessant babble and movement. Always at the start of prayer he felt scattered and distracted, and he needed courage and effort to gather himself into stillness and unity. But once he arrived at that stillness, prayer unfolded naturally, almost by itself.

## The Impact of Moods

Michael Paul learned how to find the freedom of the true self through the teaching of St Ignatius. We saw earlier how Ignatius underlined the importance of becoming aware of the conflict of moods inside us in order to have some sense of where the battle lines are. At this point, it's important to distinguish between moods and feelings or emotions. Feelings come and go quite rapidly, but moods last longer, and can be harder to eliminate. Moods are also vaguer and less specific than emotions. Feelings are sharper, often centred on a person or an event, while moods are much less focused and much more generalised. When we first become aware of them, we can feel intimidated by the intensity of our negative moods, but in reality, as Michael Paul discovered, these dark moods are somewhat like weeds in a garden. With a certain amount of vigilance, they can be kept in check, and the flowers can bloom.

Moods have a significant impact on our freedom, because they affect the three powers of our souls: the memory, the understanding and the will. Moods affect our memory, because when we are in a good mood, we easily call to mind the positive things in our past. When we're in a bad mood, on the other hand, we easily dwell on our negative memories, and these in turn can darken our mood even more. Crucially, however, the more we become aware of the bad mood, the weaker is its grip on us. Awareness makes a welcome difference.

Moods affect our understanding also. Being in a good mood enhances our thinking process, while bad moods make even the process of thinking become strenuous. What's more, bad moods can easily induce us to make mistaken judgements.

Finally, moods affect the will. We know from our own experience that when we're in a good mood, most things seem possible and we're willing to give them a go. The opposite is true for us when we are in a bad mood: even something relatively straightforward can seem difficult and demanding.

### Awareness

Awareness is already a big help, but awareness doesn't come easily. We frequently have to be jolted out of our normal patterns and rhythms to become aware of the deeper realities. We have to undergo an experience somewhat analogous to that of Ignatius in Loyola, whose enforced convalescence over a period of months woke him up to the superficiality of what he had previously held dear. William Desmond, an Irish philosopher with whose thought Michael Paul became familiar during the last decade of his life, points to Dostoevsky's experience as another example. Having been sentenced to death for alleged subversive activities, Dostoevsky was pardoned moments before the execution was to take place. He later described his reaction at that moment of reprieve: 'The sweetness of the morning air struck him, the song of morning birds, the sky. He was stunned into astonishment'. For ourselves, too, awareness usually arises only when something shakes us out of our complacency – not necessarily a shattered leg, or months in bed, or a reprieve from death, but something that interrupts our well-established patterns in an expected way.

We are unlikely to set out on a journey toward freedom unless we realise that we're not free. As Plato pointed out over two thousand years ago, prisoners can be quite content in a shadowy cave. We usually need some kind of cannonball moment to wake us up. But that is not sufficient in itself; we also need some reflective time afterwards, some space where the pace of life enables us to ponder our experience and get in touch with our real selves. And until we get in touch with our own inner life, we won't be able to arrive at the freedom of faith. The only reliable starting point for the journey into faith is awareness of the mystery within that sets the true self free.

Karl Rahner was once asked how he could still believe in God despite the huge suffering and injustice in our world. 'I believe', he said, 'because I pray.' It is a startling reversal. We normally suppose that people pray because they first believe, but Rahner here says exactly the reverse: it is because he prays that he believes. Prayer comes first, and faith follows. The implication is that ceasing to pray sooner or later means no longer believing.

Even after fully recovering from his battle wounds, St Ignatius forever stayed faithful to his convalescence experience, by prayerfully reflecting twice a day – at noon and in the evening before going to bed – on what had been happening in his day. In order to become aware of the movements of their hearts, he insisted that his fellow Jesuits do the same. Ignatius realised that we are at once drawn to freedom and lured away from it. The purpose of the daily prayerful sifting of our inner moods is to cooperate as much as we can with the movements that draw us toward goodness, truth and beauty, and ultimately toward God, and to disempower the movements that draw us in the opposite direction.

For people who imagine God as distant and removed from their lives, it can come as a shock even to entertain the notion that God might be active right now in their hearts. But that is exactly what Ignatius is saying. God is present in our lives, he says, so that God is gently speaking to us always. All we need is to learn how to tune into God's wavelength, just as Michael Paul as a young boy tuned into the stations on the family's wireless. With a little care and a little growth in freedom, we can become aware of the movements inside.

### Discernment and Freedom

The fruits of the Holy Spirit, according to St Paul (*Gal 5:22-23*), are peace, joy, love, patience, kindness and gentleness. 'Consolation', according to St Ignatius, is an attraction drawing us towards them. 'Desolation', on the other hand, draws us in the opposite direction – towards jealousy, disagreements, antagonisms and selfishness. When these two attractions come into conflict, we encounter inner turbulence, but Ignatius is confident that if we persevere consolation and joy will win out. A Christian is meant to be a person of peace and joy, and if we live out of this fundamental sense of peace then our big decisions in life will be balanced and mature.

Ignatius wants us to exploit our good moods as much as possible. The best time to make decisions and undertake challenging tasks is when our mood is positive. When we're in desolation, on the other hand, and feeling weighed down, we are easily daunted by the difficulties we face; preoccupied with our negative feelings, our decisions are less reliable and our actions less enduring. For Ignatius, the most important context for cultivating consolation and undermining desolation is gratitude; living in the certainty of God's endless generosity and care is the soil in which consolation can flourish.

Michael Paul used a lot of words to describe this key reality of discernment, this gift of recognising God's inner invitations to freedom that are being gently voiced in the movements toward peace and joy in our hearts. Yet, despite the profusion of words, he also realised that this reality was ultimately quite simple and straightforward. Sometimes our words can make things appear more complex than they really are. In this connection, Michael Paul liked to tell a story against himself.

## *Finding His Own Voice*

It was an amusing and slightly embarrassing incident that occurred while he was a student of theology. It involved the saintly Irish Jesuit to whom I briefly alluded in Chapter One. Fr John Hyde SJ was one of Michael Paul's professors when he was a student at the Milltown Institute in Dublin. He was revered as a holy man as well as a learned one, someone who had little time for unnecessary complexity. He taught Michael Paul a course on grace, which involved a fifteen-minute oral exam at the end.

Michael Paul had studied well for this exam and felt quite confident. After questioning him at length, and seeing that Michael Paul knew the various topics well, Fr Hyde asked an apparently simple question: 'What does grace do to a person?' In his reply, Michael Paul drew on the perspectives of various eminent theologians: Augustine, Aquinas, Rahner and so on. But none of his answers impressed Fr Hyde. He kept interrupting him with the same question, 'What does grace *do* to a person?' After what seemed like an eternity, the fifteen minutes were up. 'You know many things', said Fr Hyde with a little hint of irony, 'but your problem is that you never go for the jugular.' With wry satisfaction he continued, 'Grace *changes* a person. Goodbye'.

As the years passed, Michael Paul came to realise that in some ways he hadn't always gone for the jugular. He began to see that he was inclined to speak in many different voices, just as he did in his oral examination with Fr Hyde, but sometimes failed to do speak in his own voice. He liked quoting others in his writings and, being a good actor, he enjoyed imitating the style of professors he admired in his teaching. As time went by, however, he saw that there was something artificial in this approach, and that he communicated better when he had the courage to speak in his own voice.

With this insight, he found himself much more comfortable in his own skin in the later years of his teaching life – and his listeners came to relish even more his skills of communication and his profound wisdom. As he himself wrote in his final book, *Into Extra Time*, 'One of the Ten Commandments says not to "covet" one's neighbour's goods, and I think this can include talents or even personality. An artist friend of mine says that the most important moment in creating a painting is to look at the frame; within this definite space you have to work. It was a huge relief for me to stop trying to be someone else, and to recognise happily the limits of my own possibilities.'

## A Time of Surrender

Becoming free entails a journey toward simplicity. There are so many things in life that we want to hold on to – a fulfilling job, economic security, supportive friends, good health, the esteem of those around us, a sound reputation, and life itself. St Ignatius points out that some of the things we desire are unhelpful attachments, and he is especially wary of those that shape all the decisions we make and effectively rule our lives. These 'disordered attachments' are big obstacles to freedom. It takes time, grace and guts to sort through the messiness of our various attachments. We struggle to let go of some of these crutches in order to embrace our deepest desires, the ones Michael Paul always encouraged people to find, the desires that come from God. By getting in touch with these desires within us, we end up making God's desires our own, and in that way we arrive at freedom.

In his spare time, Fr Hyde studied coastal erosion, above all in the area around Ballycotton, Co. Cork, where he had grown up. For many years, this part of the coastline had undergone severe erosion, with people expressing concerns about it long before the issue of climate change entered the public consciousness. Fr Hyde was fascinated by the way the ocean eroded the land, gradually changing the shape of the coastal landscape. Michael Paul once helped him locate an unpublished geography dissertation on the area of Ballycotton Bay. As Fr Hyde thanked him, this shy man of few words commented, 'Coastal erosion is like what God does to us – or should we say it's "attitude erosion"?'

Freedom demands the erosion of our rock-like ego. We spend a lot of energy and time reinforcing the ego, and it takes real surrender to let it go. The challenge is to resist the tendency to put ourselves at the centre of the world, with our own ego as the measure of all things. The ultimate goal is to become like the ocean that God is: vast, flowing, life-giving and above all free. Michael Paul, like us all, experienced the tug-of-war between wanting to keep control and being ready to surrender. He often quoted a phrase that appears in slightly different ways in two of Shakespeare's greatest tragedies. Speaking to Horatio, Hamlet says in the play of that name, 'The readiness is all'; in *King Lear* Edgar has an even more evocative version of the same phrase, 'Ripeness is all'. Readiness implies an exercise of the will. Ripeness, on the other hand, suggests something more passive: something that can't be rushed, something to be awaited, something that happens to you.

## Into Extra Time

When Michael Paul was hit by cancer for the second time in January 2015, he was faithful to the lessons he had learned in his own life and that he used in helping others. Following the shock of the diagnosis, he began to reflect on his situation, and then he started to write down his reflections. These would appear in his final, moving book, *Into Extra Time*. The act of writing gave him a sense of purpose during this difficult period, and helped him structure his days. It also offered him the prospect of continuing, to the end, to support others in their life's search.

Even though he suffered a lot because of his cancer and the treatment he had to undergo over the final months of his life, Michael Paul grew in the conviction that God's way of 'attitude erosion' is as sensitive and gentle as possible. For this reason, he took issue with one of his favourite authors, Flannery O'Connor, perhaps for the first time ever. He disagreed with her claim that conversion involves a kind of existential earthquake, 'a blasting annihilating light', as she calls it. Michael Paul discovered through his own experience that God typically works in a much more considerate manner.

Michael Paul loved the scene in St Luke's Gospel (*Lk 5:4-11*) where the disciples have returned despondent from an unsuccessful night's fishing. At the suggestion of Jesus they reluctantly cast their nets out once more, only to haul ashore the greatest catch of their lives. At that moment, Peter throws himself at the knees of Jesus and cries, 'Depart from me, for I am a sinful man'. Michael Paul was intrigued that Peter would say something so unexpected at such a moment. A word of thanks or praise would have seemed more suitable in the circumstances. On reflection, however, it dawned upon him that there is no better moment for acknowledging sin than when we are in the presence of life in all its fullness and wonder. In the marvel of the full catch, we can accept our weakness and vulnerability. On the other hand, without God's reassuring presence, any kind of darkness – whether of sin or of suffering – can be truly frightening.

If that story had ended with Jesus doing what Peter had asked, it would have been bad news, not only for Peter, but also for all of us who become aware of our fragility and brokenness. But Jesus doesn't walk away from Peter. Even though Peter feels he has nothing to offer, Jesus can make more out of that nothingness than Peter could ever imagine. Peter is now ready to engage in a different kind of fishing – for human beings. In this new kind of fishing, however, Peter will need to remember that it won't be his own power that will energise him, but rather the inexhaustible fullness of God.

## Eternity Begins Now

In his final months and weeks, as the cancer took a serious hold of him, Michael Paul was acutely aware of his own weakness. Yet he kept saying his unsteady and often pain-filled 'yes' to God's huge and prior 'yes' to him. He returned love for love.

The Presbyterian theologian, Frederick Buechner, has a stunning insight into vocation: 'The place God calls you is the place where your deep gladness and the world's deep hunger meet'. Michael Paul's 'deep gladness' was to enter intuitively and imaginatively into the experiences of others, and to open up a space of freedom for them. He found in countless people a 'deep hunger' to be relieved of their burden of guilt and to be liberated from the blockages that shut them in upon themselves. He believed that, if this burden can be lifted and this blockage cleared, they can get in touch with the hidden gem inside, and arrive at a freedom that makes faith possible and fruitful. In this way, Michael Paul's deep gladness was to respond generously to the world's deep hunger. He also responded to a need he perceived in theology today, to go beyond a merely conceptual approach to faith, and instead to develop something much more enriching: a lived spirituality of faith.

Because he understood himself and knew his own struggles, Michael Paul could also see beyond the fragility of others to discover their hidden treasure. His facility for finding mystery at the heart of ordinary lives echoes the words of G. K. Chesterton, 'The world will never starve for want of wonders, but for want of wonder. We should always endeavour to wonder at the permanent thing, not at the mere exception. We should be startled by the sun, and not by the eclipse. We should wonder less at the earthquake, and wonder more at the earth. What was wonderful about childhood is that anything in it was a wonder. It was not merely a world full of miracles; it was a miraculous world.'

Michael Paul lived in that world. His thought and his life are an encouragement to us to take our desires and our imagination seriously, because these provide privileged openings to the greatest wonder of all – God's presence within us. He urges us to attune ourselves to the neglected wavelength of that astonishing reality, our inner world and its hidden depths. He would no doubt have agreed with the ancient philosopher Heraclitus, 'Even if you went in search of it, you would not find the boundaries of the soul though you travelled every road, so deep is its measure'. There is a profound mystery inside each one of us, more than we can fathom. In death, as in life, Michael Paul helps us to connect with this mystery, expressed so simply by the Psalmist: 'I thank you for the wonder of my being' (*Ps 139:14*).

It is surely appropriate to finish with Michael Paul's own words, written on 19 January 2015 in the section 'A Cancer Diary' of his final book, published posthumously:

> I am struck by something so obvious. The world goes on without me and will go on without me. So who knows me except God? There is an unreachable aloneness, a core of each person where only God enters to love and create. It is a space of secret, often invisible, belonging or intimacy, where nothing is without meaning, where eternity begins now, where all is being embraced in love.
> **Into Extra Time**